Moving Forward

Program for a Participatory Economy

Michael Albert

Edinburgh   London   San Francisco

Moving Forward: Program for a Participatory Economy
ISBN 1 902593 41 3

Library of Congress Catalog-in-Publication data:
A catalog record for this title is available from the Library of Congress.

British Library Cataloguing-in-Publication data:
A catalogue record for this title is available from the British Library.

Published by AK Press

P.O. Box 40682   P.O. Box 12766
San Francisco, CA   Edinburgh, Scotland
94140-0682   EH8 9YE

Cover design by John Yates.

Dedication

For Lori Berenson, Mumia Abu Jamal,
Leonard Peltier, and every human soul
in any country, on any continent,
locked in any institutional quarters
too confining to flourish

Acknowledgements

This book grew out of a series of commentaries
written for the ZNet Sustainer Program.
I thank all those who participate in that program
as writers, readers, contributors, activists, and
donors. The ideas in Moving Forward *arise from*
the work and thoughts of too many people to credit
them all, save for my frequent co-author Robin
Hahnel, jointly responsible for the participatory
economic vision, and my frequent critics and
advisors on matters of editorial content and
expression, Stephen Shalom, Cynthia Peters,
Brian Dominick, and Lydia Sargent.

Table Of Contents

Introduction

It's a poor sort of memory that only works backward.
-Cheshire Cat

Ring out old shapes of foul disease, Ring out the
narrowing lust for gold; Ring out the thousand
wars of old. Ring in the thousand years of peace.
-Alfred North Tennyson

Great social movements need long-run goals for inspiration and guidance and need short-run programs for immediate orientation and agenda. This was true for the abolitionist movement to end slavery in the nineteenth century, for the movement for women's suffrage at the turn of the century, for the labor movement that led to the CIO in the 1930s, for the civil rights, student, and peace movements seeking to expand justice in the 1960s, and for the women's liberation movement in the 1970s. It will be no less true for a 21st century movement to replace greedy competition with equitable cooperation.*Movement for a Participatory Economy* hopes to help a new economic movement settle on needed long-run goals and short-run programs by highlighting four areas of visionary and strategic concern:

- how people should be remunerated

- how decisions should be made

- how workplaces should be organized, and

- how the economy should settle on what is produced and consumed.

1

About a third of this book describes institutions to accomplish these functions consistent with desirable moral and social aspirations. Another third explores demands for nonreformist reforms that can improve our lives today and which will also propel our future goals. The remaining third uses an informal question and answer format to elaborate the picture. The thirds are not sequential, but intermixed. For each main topic addressed we provide visionary argument, question and answer, and program. The result, I hope, is a vision and program to reduce economic hierarchies of wealth, income, and influence to a minimum, or none at all.

The name of the vision is participatory economics, or for short, parecon. It is an economy based on remunerating people according to effort and sacrifice, council democracy, what we call balanced job complexes, and allocation via participatory planning. Beyond producing and distributing to fulfill human needs and expand human capacities, the values pursued are solidarity, equity, self- management, and diversity. Below we provide a brief introduction to these issues preparatory to the chapters to come.

Just Rewards

> *Hear me people: We now have to deal with another*
> *race—small and feeble when our fathers first met them,*
> *but now great and overbearing. Strangely enough they*
> *have a mind to till the soil and the love of possessions is a*
> *disease with them. They take their tithes from the*
> *poor and weak to support the rich and those who rule.*
> *-Chief Sitting Bull*

In any economy people get income that in turn determines how much they can consume relative to others. But how much should each person get in a desirable economy? Or, more formally, what should be our norm for remuneration? According to participatory economics...

- A good economy should remunerate only effort and sacrifice, not profit, power, or output.

But why should we want Bill Gates to lose his vast wealth and then earn income only for for how hard the actual work he does is, but not for having contributed to the creation of a vast and profitable enterprise? And why should we want surgeons and coal miners or hospital orderlies to earn only for the time they work and for how hard they work and how much sacrifice is involved, but not for the number of lives they save or for the tons of coal they extract or bedpans they deal with, much less for the power they are able to wield in negotiations?

Chapters one through three make a case for reward based only on effort and sacrifice, consider how to institutionally implement such a condition in a new economy, and discuss how we can get to that point. As near-term program, they explore enhancing affirmative action; increasing taxes on profit, property, wealth, inheritance, and income; undertaking job actions for increased wages; and winning a full employment program, minimum wage supports, increased social wage payments, and reverse income taxes.

Self-Management

> *Power operates only destructively, bent always on forcing every manifestation of life into the straitjacket of its laws. Its intellectual form of expression is dead dogma, its physical form brute force.*
> *-Rudolf Rocker*

Economies involve countless decisions that affect people's lives. Who should make such decisions, with how much say, and by what means? In contemporary societies corporate owners and other corporate leaders and high government officials have vast economic power. Remaining citizens simply follow orders, having little impact on major outcomes. Participatory economics seeks, instead...

- That all people should have a say in decisions proportionate to the degree they are affected by them, i.e. self-management.

But why remove current power differentials and seek self-management in their place? Why shouldn't we instead aim for "economic freedom" that gives everyone the right to do whatever they wish with themselves and their property? Or why shouldn't we give everyone equal say over all economic decisions? Or why shouldn't we give the more knowledgeable or more successful more say?

Pondering these questions, chapters four through six defend self-management as our decision-making goal, propose institutions to achieve it, and explore strategic ways to achieve those future institutions including strategies to create workers' and consumers' councils, ideas for changes in workplace decision-making procedures, and demands to replace private decision-making over collective consumption with democratic procedures that increase consumers' power.

Dignified Work

> *Wonder each morning how you're going to hold on till evening, each Monday how you'll make it to Saturday. Reach home without the strength to do anything but watch TV, telling yourself you'll surely die an idiot ... Long to smash everything... once a day, feel sick ... Because you've traded your life for a living; fear that the rage mounting within you will die down in the end, that in the final analysis people are right when they say: "ah, you can get used to anything."*
> *-Andre Gorz*

Nowadays some folks suffer harsh unemployment, not working at all. Others suffer degrading conditions and have no say in what they do. Still others have plush jobs, uplifting conditions, and overwhelming say about their own work and even over how other people's work is defined and done. If that distribution of work isn't fair, what should we seek instead? What should be the distribution of tasks so that each actor has a fair job situation? What constitutes dignified work?

- Participatory economics argues that dignified work requires each worker to have a collection of responsibilities which utilize his or her potentials and incorporate a fair share of empowering and fulfilling as well as rote and onerous labor.

Chapters seven through nine argue that every worker should enjoy comparable quality of life and empowerment effects in their work—a "balanced job complex"—for the sake of equity and self-management. Dignifying work means giving each worker a fair mix of uplifting as well as deadening labor to eliminate class division between those monopolizing empowering work and those isolated from decision-making options. These chapters counter fears that such a choice will reduce output by diminishing expertise, and they present demands to improve conditions now and lead toward balanced job complexes in the future, including compensating those with less desirable work with time off to get further schooling to attain better circumstances, requiring those with more desirable jobs to spend compensating time doing onerous work, and changing workplace relations to reduce disparities in desirability and empowerment between different jobs by reallocating tasks among them.

Participatory Allocation

Annual income twenty pounds, annual expenditure nineteen pounds and six, result happiness Annual income twenty pounds, annual expenditures twenty pounds ought and six, result misery.
-Charles Dickens

In any conceivable economy, different groups of workers make different products and some procedure for coordinating their activities with each other and with the desires of consumers is required. This procedure, called allocation, determines how much of each input and output is used or produced and where it winds up. Partly allocation depends on decisions that Tom or Jane make to do this or that. But partly allocation depends on the information, communication, and behavioral roles that impact what actors can even conceive to want to do.

Currently allocation is overwhelmingly based either on markets (for example, between corporations and between producers and consumers), or on top-down planning (for example within corporations and in the government sector). In the market interactions, producers and consumers relate to one another as adversaries. Competitive pressures drive them to take advantage of one another or be replaced by those who will. In the planned interactions, orders come from on high, authoritatively, enforcing obedience from below.

Why do people accept that acceding to the economics of competition and greed with markets or to the economics of authority and subordination with top-down planning, are the only ways workers and consumers can coordinate related activities and enjoy the advantages of a division of labor? Instead, why can't we consciously and democratically plan our efforts while cooperating equitably and efficiently?

In response to these questions, chapters ten through twelve explain how workers and consumers can allocate scarce productive resources and distribute valuable goods and services without markets or central planning. Participatory economics...

• Advocates a decentralized, social planning procedure called "participatory planning" in which workers' and consumers' councils propose and revise their own activities in socially responsible ways.

These three chapters summarize the advantages of participatory planning over both markets and central planning, explain why fears that such participatory planning would prove inefficient or limit legitimate freedoms are misplaced, and discuss demands for restricting the influence of market forces and expanding the role of equitable cooperation, including banning involuntary overtime, reducing the workweek, imposing tax and budget reforms, and expanding public influence over investment and budget decisions.

We Don't Live by Bread Alone

The planet has—or rather had—a problem,
which was this: most of the people on it
were unhappy for pretty much of the time.
Many solutions were suggested for the problem,
but most of these were largely concerned
with the movements of small green pieces
of paper, which is odd because
on the whole it wasn't the small
green pieces of paper that were unhappy.
-Douglas Adams

Economics is not the only social function important to social interaction. Among other central facets of social life are how we define cultural communities and their identities, how we accomplish kinship related functions having to do with the birth and socialization of the next generation, and how we accomplish political functions of legislation, adjudication, and implementation and enforcement of collective agreements. A desirable economy must, of course, mesh with our ways of organizing the rest of social life. Likewise, how we organize other parts of social life must mesh with whatever choices we make for our economy.

In chapters thirteen and fourteen, we address this two-way requirement and explore some implications of favoring participatory economics for other domains of life. We look specifically at education, race, gender, ecology, the state, and international relations.

Participatory Economic Program and Vision

> *The task for a modem industrial society is to achieve*
> *what is now technically realizable, namely, a*
> *society which is really based on free voluntary*
> *participation of people who produce and create, live*
> *their lives freely within institutions they control, and with*
> *limited hierarchical structures, possibly none at all.*
> *-Noam Chomsky*

Movements need a broad and varied program, but also centrally highlighted campaigns. In chapters fifteen and sixteen we discuss a campaign that could become a programmatic centerpiece for a Movement for a Participatory Economy in the twenty-first century. The focus includes demands for a short work-week with wage and income features that maximize the benefits. We explore the demand's implications for immediate improvement in people's quality of life, but also for consciousness-raising and organizational gains that would empower new movements to win further advances in the future.

Motivating Vision and Strategy

> *True compassion is more than flinging a coin*
> *at a beggar; it comes to see that an edifice*
> *which produces beggars needs restructuring.*
> *-Martin Luther King Jr.*

> *"Incapacity of the masses." What a tool for all*
> *exploiters and dominators, past, present, and future...*
> *-Voline*

Demands we choose in the present and tactics we employ to try to win them should of course reduce current suffering but they should also move us toward long-run goals, augmenting our strengths and reducing those of our opponents. Today's efforts should increase the number of people seeking change, increase the understanding and commitment of advocates of change, strengthen dissident organizations and means of outreach and struggle, and generally win gains that not only improve the lot of suffering constituencies, but also empower them to win further gains and become ever more committed and capable tomorrow. These simple norms are central to social strategy. Having visionary goals and relating our programs for action to them can help highlight current injustices, spur our motivations, and orient our actions toward achieving a more equitable and free society.

Nonetheless, many advocates of social change feel that offering institutional vision and strategy can hurt activism. Not wanting to ignore such views about the undesirability of this book's agenda, to close this introduction we briefly offer a hypothetical critic of elaborating vision plus a "pareconist" reply.

Dialogue On the Value of Vision

Just now I want to tell you why the worker does not take the burglar by the neck and kick him out: that is, why he begs the capitalist for a little more bread or wages, and why he does not throw him off his back altogether. It is because the worker, like the rest of the world, has been made to believe that everything is all right and must remain as it is; and that if a few things are not quite as they should be, then it is because "people are bad" and everything will right itself in the end, anyhow.
-Alexander Berkman

On this issue of human freedom, if you assume that there's no hope, you guarantee there will be no hope. If you assume that there is an instinct for freedom, that there are opportunities to change things, that hope is possible, then hope may be justified, and a better world may be built.
—Noam Chomsky

CRITIC: A blueprint approach to winning change has fared badly over and over in history, leading repeatedly to unjust and inequitable ends. We shouldn't have a blueprint, because blueprints lead to bad ends.

PARECONIST: Who is suggesting a blueprint? At present, we don't even have a generally shared workable outline of what we desire. When we are asked what we want to replace capitalism, we have nothing constructive, worthy, and viable to offer. So it isn't a nuts and bolts blueprint we are advocating, but a broad understanding of new institutions to inform our dissent, guide our demands and actions, and provide hope for what we can attain.

As to "the blueprint approach having fared badly," I'm not sure what you mean. Every country with movements against capitalism that has sought a vision and won significant change has in fact got what they sought. So having a vision didn't preclude arriving at what the vision outlines. Quite the contrary, it makes that highly likely. Having a vision doesn't make one ineffective, though I agree that having a bad vision yields bad outcomes. If the people holding a vision aren't the whole movement but are only narrow elites, and if the vision they hold serves them but not the broad movement, then, yes, I agree that's a serious problem.

CRITIC: But no one can possibly know the future well enough to provide vision beyond mere guesswork or wishful thinking.

PARECONIST: I agree that no one can draw a detailed picture of of some new society or economy. But we can conceive viable, desirable, alternative institutions with positive implications, and struggle to implement those. And in fact, having that much vision is the only way to build movements that aren't purely reactive, reformist, and/or vague, and that incorporate the hope and clarity essential to long-term commitment.

CRITIC: But it is hard enough to agree on short-term reform demands in our movements. It would be impossible for us to agree on a blueprint—and since we're nowhere close to agreeing, why gnash our teeth over it, wasting time that could go to constructive organizing work?

PARECONIST: But what if one reason it is hard to agree on the short-term is because we have little clarity about the long-term, not a blueprint, but a viable vision? And what if it will actually be pretty easy to agree on a broad workable and desirable goal, once we actually try to do so, and that having arrived at one, the context and orientation it provides will make it easier to arrive at effective short-term preferences?

CRITIC: Okay, maybe we need something, but why not just our values as compared to capitalist or market values: solidarity, democracy, participation, liberty, diversity, egalitarianism, people over profit, protecting the weak. Why can't that be our glue and our source of hope and direction? Why bother with institutional details?

PARECONIST: Values are crucial, of course, but without advocating associated institutions that implement them, values tend to become rhetorical. For example, Clinton can espouse the values you listed, even people over profits. And certainly Leninists and other advocates of authoritarian outcomes can mouth the values you listed, with great and sincere feeling. Without institutional substance, the values alone don't get us far, and the populace is astute enough to know that. Any value you care to enunciate can find its way into a Madison Avenue jingle overnight. But an institutional vision that precludes the existence of Madison Avenue—that's another matter.

So I agree with you that we want egalitarianism—but does that mean people get paid according to output, or according to effort and sacrifice, or what? And how is the payment to be accomplished? And why should anyone believe that it can be accomplished, supposing we do describe a method?

And I agree that we want participation and democracy, but does that mean we have a typical corporate division of labor with a two-party government, or do we have workers' councils with markets or with central planning, or do we have something very different, such as self-managing councils with balanced job complexes linked by a new kind of allocation? And how does what we seek actually operate? With what impact? Values support and inform vision, but they are not its entirety.

CRITIC: This is all so abstract. You have logical answers, sure, but ultimately the vision stuff just doesn't interest me. It's just not relevant to my real life.

PARECONIST: I am not sure what you mean by not relevant to your life. You want to win change and a better world. So isn't "the vision stuff" relevant to your life if it could help you do that, and not relevant if it can't?

On a more immediate and personal level, is your life impacted in some way by some project or institution of the left? If so, does that project or institution have a corporate structure or does it have a participatory structure? Wouldn't it be relevant to you if a movement advocated egalitarian, participatory structures in substantive institutional terms, not only for society, but for its own institutions?

Before the women's movement, lots of people argued that feminism wasn't relevant for most activists. But when women made redefining the social relations between men and women part of what being on the left meant, feminism became directly relevant to everyone involved in social change, not just in terms of goals and broad strategies or demands, but for how movements are organized now—for their culture, their decision-making, the lives of men and women in them. In other words, the espousal of feminist vision and aims impacted not only the broad agenda of the left, but also the daily life situation of activists. Similarly, an economic vision worthy of support will impact not only broad left goals and strategies, but also how our current institutions handle money, divisions of labor, and decision making and allocation, and thus how they impact our activist work, whatever its form may be.

CRITIC: Social struggle has to begin with acting in the world and to continually arise from that. It shouldn't involve going off in a study group to figure out what you're for.

PARECONIST: Why does developing and espousing goals violate the notion that our thoughts should be based in experience? Nobody is suggesting that we should have utopian goals divorced from reality. Of course every new experience is valuable, but how long does one have to engage in direct actions before one advocates a vision that one's direct actions are sup-posed to lead toward? Do you have to be an activist for one, ten, thirty, or two hundred years? If thirty or less, then we are there already, even just personally. If it's a hundred or more, then the movement is there, as a collective entity.

CRITIC: But if you argue there's nothing you can do but over-throw capitalism, then since everyone can see that the over-throw of capitalism is far off, you're basically telling them there's nothing they can do.

PARECONIST:: Well, we don't know how far off it is, do we...but why does having a goal imply there is nothing one can do but win the full goal by overthrowing capitalism? We don't think any such thing. Instead, there is plenty to be done now, of course, but having a goal facilitates being able to develop and organize around effective short-term program.

On the other hand, if you rage against profits and injustice indicating that the problem we all suffer is capitalism, but then you have no answer for what comes after capitalism, you implicitly legitimate the capitalist's claim that there is no al-ternative. By forgoing institutional goals, you imply that capi-talism is permanent. The lesson many people will take from your lack of answers for what you want beyond capitalism, will be that resilient capitalism will swamp any social victo-ries we may temporarily attain.

But there is no such problem if we clearly and accessibly say here is what would be much better than capitalism, and here are things that can be won today and that can improve our lives now and that can also be part of a sequence of changes that lead toward this new system. Then we can have a long-term goal that sustains and gives us hope and orienta-tion, plus a short-term program to fight for now.

CRITIC: It sounds nice, the way you hope for it to happen, but in practice enunciating long-term goals leads to a kind of reli-gious movement, disconnected from reality. I won't be strate-gic due to its rigidity and will suffer all kinds of sectarian splits because it's focused on rhetoric without consequences.

PARECONIST: Can that happen? Sure. Is it horrible? Yes. But does it have to happen? No. So to prevent it we shouldn't dispense with something that we need, but should instead formulate vision that explicitly guards against arrogance and sectarianism and is publicly owned by everyone in the movement, and couched in clear language so everyone can understand it and make it their own, including adapting and improving it. Without that, it isn't that there won't be vision—but that the vision that does exist will be held by narrow elites and service only elites, not everyone.

So we have a great irony: The only way to have vision that is non-sectarian and anti-elitist, isn't for good people who are concerned about these abuses to foreswear vision so that people who aren't concerned privately generate and later implement harmful vision. The solution is for people with good concerns to articulate vision in a public dialogue so it arises from and is possessed by those most in need of change, and is imbued with desirable values. This process is not divorced from reality, as you fear, but will instead have profound immediate implications. For example, sharing the economic vision in this volume, activists would agree that left institutions should be participatory and democratically restructured; they should have balanced job complexes, just remuneration, self management, etc. This internal change would profoundly affect the class attitudes, policies, and consciousness of our movements, and their membership composition as well.

An Invitation

> *It is no longer enough to point out what we don't like,*
> *we have to work out 'what sort of society we do want'...*
> *-Sheila Rowbotham*

Books can convey information, arguments, logic, and evidence, but cannot facilitate back and forth exchange. Nowadays elements of such exchange are possible and even easy, due to new technologies of communication— and we welcome readers to please visit the Participatory Economics web site at http://www.parecon.org—a component of ZNet—which is at http://www.zmag.org. The parecon site has much additional information, exploring matters raised here and other issues as well, including some books online, many essays and debate exchanges, plus a way to pursue direct debate and mutual communication with the authors and with other people interested in participatory economic vision and movement in what we call online forums.

1. Just Rewards

*My own hopes and intuitions are that
self-fulfilling and creative work is a fundamental
human need, and that the pleasures of a challenge
met, work well done, the exercise of skill and
craftsmanship, are real and significant, and are
an essential part of a full and meaningful life.*
-Noam Chomsky

In any economy the collective efforts of all workers create the economic product. Imagine the total product as a gigantic apple pie. What size piece do you get for your particular labors? What do I get for mine? What determines everyone's income, or how much pie we can each have? In fancier language, what is the economy's norm for remuneration?

In capitalist economies people are remunerated profits for how much property they own and remunerated wages or bonuses for how much power they have or what they can negotiate or extort for the output they generate. Would we retain all these norms for remuneration—property, power, output— in a good economy, or would we eliminate one or more? And is there any other norm that we would add?

Rewarding Property?

*We can have democracy or we can have the concentration of
wealth in the hands of a few. We cannot have both.*
- Supreme Court Justice Louis Brandeis

Possession is 9/10 of the problem.
-John Lennon

It is unlikely that many folks reading this brief visionary and strategic book think that people should be rewarded for owning property. Rewards for property are called profit... wherein individuals who own the means of production pocket profits based on the output of those means of production. You own some machines. The machines have high output that can be sold for revenues that exceed the costs of maintaining them. You pocket the difference, or profit. You needn't do anything other than keep track of your deed to your property, while sipping mint juleps, or dry martinis.

This leads to someone like Bill Gates (whose profit income in no way depends on his labors but only on his stock portfolio) having more wealth than the entire GNP of 5 Central American countries combined, or, if you prefer, 475 billionaires together having more wealth than half the world's population. But rewarding property ownership not only leads to grotesquely exorbitant differentials of wealth and power that distort virtually all dimensions of social life, it also, even when not so exorbitant, doesn't reward a person for something morally worthy that he or she has done, nor even provide the most compelling incentives to do something desirable that he or she otherwise might not have done.

We inherit or amass property overwhelmingly due to luck in the parent lottery, or luck or guile in competition. We can't change anything regarding who our parents are and how much property they have to leave us. We are born to whom we are born. If we get lucky and happen to get a grip on a company that in turn gets a grip on a huge piece of a market yielding big or even gargantuan profits...rewarding us with a huge swath of it is surely not morally warranted, nor incentive-warranted. In fact, it isn't even what most often happens, since most often, Bill Gates aside, operations become overwhelmingly owned by investors who do nothing but move money around from project to project with the people who founded the operations and built them retaining only a very small percentage of the holdings. At any rate, rewarding property with profits says that having a deed in your pocket is a one-way ticket to vast wealth. There is no moral or economic

able that people use better tools if they are available. But do we have to provide a morally questionable reward to the person benefitting from having the better tools in order to provide economic incentive for socially optimal allocation of tools? Instead why can't we have an economy which requires sensible allocations of resources and tools and technology for remuneration to occur at all, but which doesn't then unjustly reward its actors?

Suppose Sally is very large and strong and Sam is much smaller and weaker. This time suppose they use the same tools. They again go into the fields for eight hours. They again work equally hard. They again endure the same conditions. Again Sally's pile is twice Sam's, this time due to her greater strength. Should Sally get twice Sam's income? If so, then we have rewarded her luck in the genetic lottery that gave her greater strength. Is that moral or efficient? Certainly there is no moral logic. And while we want to get appropriate levels of output from people in light of their inherited endowments, we don't have to reward the size of their output to accomplish that, we only have to remunerate for appropriate output given tools and talents, as we will see below.

To continue, suppose we compare two people doing mathematics investigations, or creating works of art, or doing surgery, or doing anything else that is socially desirable. They work equally hard under the same conditions. One has more of some relevant natural talent and the other has less of it. Should the former be rewarded commensurately more than the latter? Clearly, there is no moral reason to do so. Why reward someone for genetic luck on top of the benefits that that genetic luck already bestowed on them? The person did nothing meritorious to gain the "talented genes" in the first place. More controversially, there is also no incentive reason to reward output per se. A potential recipient of bounty paid for innate talent cannot change her natural talent in response to the promise of higher pay. Everyone's natural endowment is what it is, and being paid for output won't provide us incentive to change our genes to increase our natural endowment . We simply can't do that. There is no incentive effect on our talents of rewarding our talents. An economy does want us to utilize our talents, to be sure, but aren't there ways to accomplish that other than providing morally and socially inappropriate levels of income?

How about education or learned skills? Shouldn't improving our productivity be morally rewarded, it being a meritorious choice? And shouldn't we also want to promote such choices? That seems reasonable, and learning should be rewarded, yes, but not in proportion to the output the education permits, rather in proportion to the effort and sacrifice it required. In other words, we should always reward for the act undertaken, the oranges picked, the math problems solved, the art painted, or the schooling undertaken to enhance one's skills. And we should provide proper incentive for undertaking the productive acts, yes. But that is very different than looking at lifetime output and saying we will reward people in accord with that output.

Rewarding Only Effort and Sacrifice!

Farming looks mighty easy when your plow is a pencil, and you're a thousand miles from the corn field.
-Dwight D. Eisenhower

Suppose we reward effort and sacrifice, not property, power, or output. What happens? Well, if jobs were like now, those doing the most onerous, dangerous, or otherwise debilitating work would be highest paid per hour of normal effort. In contrast, those with the most comfortable conditions and circumstances would be lowest paid per hour of normal effort. This choice is moral in that it rewards people for putting out in their work, and/or for enduring more hardship on behalf of enlarging or improving the quality of the social product. But does rewarding only effort and sacrifice mess up the economy by distorting incentives and thereby leading to defective or diminished social product related to the assets on hand?

Put more specifically, one might ask: Shouldn't a surgeon get paid for all those years of schooling, as compared to a nurse or a janitor, who has less schooling?

Sure. The surgeon should be paid, while schooling, for whatever the level of effort and sacrifice the years of schooling entail. Later, the surgeon should be paid in accord with the effort and sacrifice expended at work, just like the janitor in the hospital should. In this event, each person should be rewarded according to the same norm—that is, paid according to effort and sacrifice expended at a worthwhile job that contributes to society.

But then "no one will be a surgeon," is the reply. Folks will prefer being a janitor because it pays more, and also why would anyone go the extra years of school to get paid less?

To see why, let's imagine you are just out of college. You now have to choose—will it be medical school for six years followed by being a doctor for forty more years, or would you prefer being a janitor in the local hospital for the full forty-six years? More exactly, how much do you have to be paid to go to medical school instead of being a janitor for the first six years, in light of the quality of life you will have during that period, and later? Or, vice versa, how much would you have to be paid to opt to be a janitor for the first six years rather than to go to medical school? And then, how much would you need to be paid to do either of the jobs, as compared to the other, for the remaining forty years?

To ask these questions is to answer them and to reveal that the motivational effects of payment according to effort and sacrifice are exactly right if we are discussing a world in which people are free to choose their jobs without encumbrances from history or from limiting institutions. Of course not everyone will seek these specific jobs, but the thought experiment is easy to translate to all other realms.

In short, other things equal and all options open, you need and deserve more pay to provide you the incentive to do that which requires greater effort and sacrifice—way more to be a janitor than a student. But you don't need nor do you deserve more pay to do something that is more fulfilling, more empowering, or yields more output, assuming it doesn't require greater effort and sacrifice. In fact, you need less to be motivated to be a doctor than a janitor.

It is a remarkable testimony to the malignant purpose, character, and affectivity of modern schooling that there is confusion about these matters. The malignant purpose is to inculcate notions and expectations consistent with maintaining social relations as they are. The malignant character is to make students passive regarding claims made by authorities. The malignant affectivity is born out by the results. So, go into any high school or college classroom. Create a relaxed and jovial tone. Announce that the average income for brain surgeons has risen to $300,000 a year. Announce that the average income for coal miners is at $60,000 a year. Describe the conditions of work for each, using coal miners of old, by the way—with black lung and risks of cave-ins, and all the rest (or you could substitute hospital orderly, janitor, sewage plant pump repair diver, sandhog, assembly line worker, etc.) Ask how many students would like a job more or less like that of the surgeon, in their preferred area, versus how many would like a job more or less like the coal miner. Then ask folks how come the surgeon's income is so high. People will answer because he or she has to go to so many more years of school, because he or she makes such a valuable contribution to society, and mostly because he or she wouldn't do that job if he or she weren't paid as an inducement.

Now there are all sorts of problems—the true answer being because the surgeons have the power to extort that pay—but for purposes in this chapter, the thing to pursue next is this. Pick any student, randomly. Tell them they are about to graduate into the workforce, or to choose to go to school for another six years. Tell them their choice...$60,000 for the coal mining or similar job for the next forty six years, or six years of school with very low income and then a few years of slowly growing salary, and then forty years at $300,000 as a surgeon, or in some similar job. Now tell them you are going to change the rates and you want to know when they will switch from opting for more schooling and the high paying (highly empowering, highly admired, better work conditions) option to the more working class option. You will have to drop the surgeon's salary well below $60,000 to get the wanna-be surgeon to prefer, instead, to go off and mine coal, if you can get them to change at all. You will be able to get the coal miner, however, to switch with no trouble, of course, even for a drop in pay rate. And in this little exercise, for those paying attention, the entire edifice of nonsensical rhetoric about needing to pay more to get people to be willing to go to school or do more pleasant and empowering work will drop away, pareconish insights rising in its place.

Just reward, both morally and regarding economic incentives as well, requires that those who put out more effort and sacrifice at a needed set of tasks for society employing capacities and resources appropriately, get more income. Those who put out less effort and sacrifice for society, get less income. Output may often reasonably be an indicator of effort, of course, but output does not itself warrant reward. (For how effort is measured, beyond by looking at results, we have to wait until we get a little further in the overall picture of allocation —but for who measures it, well, of course your peers, your workmates).

And what if someone can't exert due to health or other reasons? Even wage slave economies recognize that in such cases there ought to be remuneration anyway. Reasonable people could differ about how much there should be, of course, but if you can't work, receiving the average income so that you are not unduly gaining or losing economically due to your health, would seem proper.

And what if someone has some ailment requiring expensive treatments, or suffers some calamity—natural or otherwise—that destroys their holdings? Of course, a just society addresses these needs socially, insuring against them for everyone and not leaving individuals to suffer catastrophes alone.

And what about children who can't/shouldn't work? Are they dependent on the income of parents, so that parents with three children have less per person than those with one child or none? One can imagine various attitudes about this, the most simple being that society provides income for all children unable to work as yet, just as for anyone else who is unable to work. This income allotment is average, perhaps with variations for age, rewarded simply for being human. The income for a family, then, is the income for the adults, plus the income that goes to children through the adults.

So in light of the above examples, the remuneration norm we advocate for a desirable economy is Just Rewards, which is payment according to effort and sacrifice or according to need when effort cannot be expended or when need is excessive due to disease or other calamity.

2. Q&A: Remuneration

All who are not lunatics are agreed about certain things. That it is better to be alive than dead, better to be adequately fed than starved, better to be free than a slave. [More]...humankind has become so much one family that we cannot insure our own prosperity except by insuring that of everyone else. If you wish to be happy yourself, you must resign yourself to seeing others also happy.
-Bertrand Russell

- *How does "remuneration according to effort and sacrifice" fit in with "equity (in circumstance and income)?"*

Remuneration according to effort and sacrifice (and in some cases need) is rather different than the usual left precept—which is remuneration according to contribution to the social product. The latter pays a large person and a small person cutting cane by the size of the piles they accumulate. The former pays a large person and a small person cutting cane for the amount of time they are working (assuming they are both working comparably hard). This also goes for a person who has learned how to cut well and one who doesn't have the same competence. For the same hardship and effort, even with different size piles cut, you get the same pay.

Now suppose you have a cushy job and I have a horribly onerous one. We both work a full day, at the rate each job calls for. I would be paid more because of more hardship (and probably more effort). Thus if there is no equity of circumstance but there is pay according to effort and sacrifice, pay makes up for inequity of circumstance. If there is real equity of circumstance, then pay will be a function of time worked except for modest variation in effort.

Criticisms among progressives and leftists of paying according to effort and sacrifice are rarely that it is unjust, but that it doesn't provide a proper incentive system to get the best overall outcomes. Critics admit parecon has just work and remuneration, but assert that the total produced will drop drastically with the gain in justice. But this is typical economic dogma that falls apart under even modest scrutiny...

- *I understand that workers in parecon would be paid according to effort, but what would stop all the workers at a plant from agreeing to give each other A+ effort ratings, thus getting A+ wages?*

A good economy has to perform a somewhat delicate balancing act if it is to promote both productive efficiency and also social justice. It has to maximize socially valuable production and at the same time it has to assure that individual workers' compensation is based on effort and sacrifice rather than rewarding innate talent, luck, good-looks, etc. A participatory economy would do this in a two-step process:

Step 1: Within the workplace each worker's degree of effort is assessed by those who are in the best position to know and most fairly acknowledge it. Workers can choose lots of approaches for this—there is no single right way. They might all carefully be given a rating—like a school grade of 0%-100%, with careful gradations. At another workplace, average effort may be the assumed default, and deviations from it registered only in special cases, and with only a few grades of rating. In any event, rating is done with the understanding that the distribution of workers' effort in the workplace is accurately reflected in the distribution of ratings. (When we discuss balancing job complexes in and between workplaces to eliminate class division and create conditions for real self management, we'll see that it also has the convenient side-effect of making it much easier to measure effort and sacrifice.)

Step 2: Among workplaces, we also need to regulate the total compensation one workplace receives with what others receive. In effect, this sets an objective standard for the assignment of effort ratings. Let's say for the sake of simplicity that two councils produce the same product—organic rolled oats. If the productive resources—unrolled oats, plant, machinery, human talent, etc. and effort in each workplace is the same, then the operative assumption is that output will be the same (within a tolerable margin of error). It is the job of some office or section of the economy to keep an accurate inventory of each council's productive resources, including the relevant abilities of the workers themselves. Using this approach, if council A has 20% better productive resources than council B (holding effort constant), A is expected to produce 20% more rolled oats. Similarly, each council has a quota to meet which is set by the overall planning process, in which, of course, it participates proportionately, as we will see in later chapters. If a council makes 80% of the average, then since differences in productive resources have already been accounted for, the under-performance is attributable to what's left—effort—and each worker's rating is multiplied by 0.8. If a council makes 120% of its adjusted expected output the reason must be more exertion, more effort, so the worker gets more pay—the rating is multiplied by 1.2. This is a possible approach. There are many others. Different industries, much less different economies, can vary in this and other aspects, of course. A parecon can choose among possibilities that achieve desired outcomes depending on its priorities and on its assessment of the worth of different ways of operating.

Depending on what method is in place, yes, I suppose there could be a lot of belly-aching when it came time to review a council's productive resources and establish its output. But if the criteria for assigning these goals were determined by the people within a sector of the economy who knew it best—the workers themselves or their chosen representatives—then it would be a democratic and defensible process.

And again, the above is only one approach, not a single correct approach. A parecon might come up with other options, as might different firms and sectors within a parecon. For example, different workplaces might have more relaxed or more demanding attitudes about trying to make remuneration precisely reflect a very detailed accounting, or might (this is my personal expectation) just have it default according to hours worked, ignoring minor variations in effort in balanced job complexes, and appending ratings deviations from average only in special cases. What is accepted throughout every participatory economy, however, is the remunerative norm and the need to implement it consistently with all other defining norms of the economy—such as balanced job complexes, council democracy, self management, etc.

- *Rewarding someone according to effort and sacrifice is still fundamentally an incentive to do something you don't enjoy. What if I choose to sit at home and write poetry all day? What sort of income should I be guaranteed?*

None, if the poetry is only for you. That is, if you choose to do things that have no benefit for others , then you are saying that society should carry you because you say it ought to. There is no moral reason for that. It is called freeloading.

Think of fifty people marooned on an island. They have to make do by their labors. There is a lot of work to get done. There are also, however, fun things to do—from walks on the beach to swimming, to playing games, taking a nap, etc. Someone says, hold on, I don't want to prepare meals, or to deal with maintaining shelters, or to do anything else even a little onerous. Should the rest of the island's citizens feed that person with their labors? No, of course not. Now suppose they are there by virtue of a shipwreck and one person was hurt badly and can't work. Do we want to feed that person? Of course we do. These are the norms of parecon, trivially obvious human norms, it seems.

- *But wouldn't it be fairer to allow people to work less than the average amount if they want, or even not at all, and still get a living wage? I doubt that we'd have many peo-*

*ple do so, and requiring work for income brings to mind
some kind of moralistic form of forced labor.*

There are some problems of communication feeding this
question, I think, and then some real issues.

First, nothing in a parecon can be called "forced labor" in
any sensible interpretation of these words. Second, because
even after clarifying the above an issue still remains, the link
between effort and sacrifice and income is a bit more subtle
than you are crediting, and sundering that link has diverse
implications that you are missing.

In general, in any economy, if we look at a year's outcomes
retrospectively we can see that a certain total volume of stuff
was produced. More, the total output had a certain make up of
so much of this and so much of that, was distributed to the
population with so much going here and so much going there,
and was produced in the first place by people doing so much labor, under such and such conditions of work, with so and so
levels of impact on their circumstances.

Okay—so, in any economy we can ask how from all the possibilities that one could imagine occurring, does this one that
actually occurred get picked? The answer is always going to
involve some combination of the dynamics of the economy and
the choices of whichever actors are able to impact outcomes.

The economic visionary, therefore, has to come up with
economic institutions that yield desired human, social, personal, and material outcomes in ways that persist over time
and meet his or her moral requirements. Now,shortcutting to
the issue in contention, supposing we have for an economy (as
with any parecon) the following, among other norms:

1) Everyone receives a socially average income of items
   and services of their choosing, and those who have
   special needs for more (such as medicine) get that
   too—all by right, as citizens.

2) Everyone who is able (but not those who aren't) has a
   responsibility to work at a socially average job complex

producing socially valued outputs of his or her choosing, for a socially average length of time each month. However, if one wishes to, and if one's work situations allow for it, one can work some overtime for proportionately more than the socially average income, or somewhat less than the social average, for proportionately less than the socially average income.

3) The total volume produced, and its composition of different items, and the actual tasks and procedures undertaken, and so on and so forth, are decided via participatory planning (still to be described).

That is parecon. And now the question that we are discussing arises, should we add another norm—for example:

4) Anyone can decide for whatever reason to work less than the social average by any amount they might choose, but still receive the socially average income.

Or, alternatively—

4a) There is some income deemed "living" and anyone who wishes to, and is able, can decide not to work at all and nonetheless receive this living income by right.

Well, if we are going to decide whether to add (4) or (4a) or some other option to receive more than the effort and sacrifice you expend in work warrants, we have to determine what are the gains and losses of the proposed change. And to do that properly, we have to ask not only about one aspect or two—for example does the person who works less and gets the same amount as if they worked more feel better, but about all sides of the situation including effects on others, on social relations, on the quality of choices made in participatory planning and their trajectory, etc.

Thus, we have to state our values and ask if the proposed change, via the impact it has on all actors and on production, allocation, and consumption, and via its impact on the economy's institutions, furthers these values or not.

Now the values behind parecon (and someone might prefer some other ones, of course) are solidarity, equity (material and circumstantial), participatory self-management, and diversity. So the question becomes, does adding rule (4) or (4a) give us better results for one or more of these values via its impact on distribution, consumption, decision making, or the make up of the social product? And does it have any deleterious effects that offset these gains? And which "weighs" more?

I will tell you that when I think about this, I still think the answer is no, this kind of change not only doesn't make things better, it makes things worse, on numerous counts. The implications of (4) or (4a) on equity are to reduce it by rewarding sloth, The implications for solidarity are to reduce it, by creating resentment. The implications for participatory self-management are to diminish it, by giving non-workers more say than they should have. And the implications for diversity are not clear, at least to me. These assessments become evident the minute we pay attention not only to obvious immediate implications—that some people don't do work they prefer to avoid but get some income for it anyhow—but also its impact on the broader relations among actors.

Finally, one more point. We can think about adding a rule like (4a) at the outset, or we can think about doing it after a parecon has been in existence, without the rule, for a few generations. This is not the same, by a long shot. In the former case, we have to ask what the implications of adding the rule are for the way that different existent constituencies/classes (in present society) would view the goal, and would try to adapt it as it is being created. In the latter case, these constituencies/classes no longer exist.

- *What about contingent or part time work? Would there be anything like that in a parecon?*

In a capitalist economy the owner of each firm is pressured by their need to maximize profits to reduce payments to the workforce as much as possible, while extracting as much labor as they can from that same workforce. There are endless variations on how they do this—lengthening the work day, speeding up the pace of work, reducing the cost of conditions by spending less on comfort, safety, etc., fragmenting workers to make all the above possible, and also bypassing costs for health care, paid vacation, and other benefits whenever they can. One trick for accomplishing all this is to hire workers part time or in other reduced capacities to escape norms and laws that protect full time employees.

In a parecon, of course, none of this exists. There is no owner of a firm. No one seeks profits. There is no market-based or other pressure to exploit labor directly or indirectly—but, to see this we have to get a fuller picture of the whole system, in coming chapters.

3. Seeking Just Rewards

Much more seriously than they themselves realize,
property is their God, their only God, which long ago
replaced in their hearts the heavenly god of the Christians.
And, like the latter, in days of yore, the bourgeois are capable
of suffering martyrdom and death for the sake of this God.
-Mikhail Bakunin

Suppose that based on last chapter's core arguments and further thought and exploration we come to agree that people ought to be paid only according to how hard they work and how onerous their work conditions are. To attain these ends we must reduce and ultimately eliminate reward for property, power, and output; reduce and finally eliminate the impact of race and gender on remuner- ation; and increase reward for effort and sacrifice to appropriate levels. What kinds of demands can we implement in the present that would benefit deserving constituencies now, and also move us toward Just Rewards in the long run?

Income Redistribution

For every dollar the boss has and didn't work for, one of us
worked for a dollar and didn't get it.
-Big Bill Haywood

At the extreme, people like Bill Gates earn many millions per day, from profits on capital. Below Gates and others like him, a few percent in the U.S. economy receive millions per month or year from capital. Next down, about 20 percent of the population monopolize most productive skills, decision- making levers, and other variables that enhance bargaining power in wage negotiations. At the high end of this group we find athletes and movie stars who can earn many millions of dollars yearly. More typically we find folks who monopolize the levers of day-to-day decision making and largely control and define their own work conditions and pace and that of others—including doctors, lawyers, managers, high level engineers, and elite university faculty—and who earn yearly incomes ranging from roughly $100,000 to $500,000 and sometimes much more. It is hard to figure an average for this "coordinator class," but $200,000 yearly is indicative. Beneath these folks, we find working people, and then the unemployed poor.

The top one percent of the population holds about 40% of the U.S. wealth. Bill Gates alone has (or had at the time of this writing) just a bit more wealth than Zimbabwe, Ghana, Iceland, Panama, Costa Rica, Kenya, El Salvador, and the Dominican Republic combined. The next 9% holds another 33% of the wealth, so that all together the top 10% holds just under three-quarters of the wealth of the U.S.. The next 10% holds about 11.5% of U.S. wealth (which is to say these folks have more or less an average share each). The next 40% of the population holds about 15% of the wealth. The last 40% holds all together about one half a percent, essentially, nothing. Similarly, the average pay in the top twenty percent is about eight times the average in the bottom 40%. The average pay in the top 1% is over 30 times the average in the bottom 40%. And in the really high echelons, the average U.S. CEO made 209 times the pay of factory workers in 1996.

Our first demands for Just Rewards aim to redistribute income or wealth from the capitalist and coordinator/managerial classes either to the general social good or directly to the most needy in society. Here are some worthy focuses.

Profit taxes

Profit taxes take wealth that ought not accrue to some folks and return it to the social pot, thereby reducing excessive disparities. The ultimate demand is a 100% profit tax since profit does not reward effort or sacrifice and we have decided that effort and sacrifice (and need when appropriate) are all that should justify income. However, in addition to an ultimate goal, we need short-term demands attainable in the present. It is like building a skyscraper: You don't erect girders for the top floors before you lay them for the lower floors. The first tasks in creating a skyscraper need to provide a foundation for those that come later, and likewise winning short-term economic demands needs to reward deserving constituencies and also strengthen their dissent and empower them to win more gains in the future. A movement for a participatory economy might sensibly demand a 50% profit tax, fighting for it in a manner that explains why profits per se are misguided tools of economic distribution.

Wealth, Inheritance, and Luxury Goods Taxes

A wealth tax makes it hard to retain great wealth. An inheritance tax makes it hard to bequeath great wealth to offspring. A luxury tax takes a cut whenever someone buys something beyond what most people can afford. Again, a 100% inheritance tax above some modest level makes moral sense, as does a high wealth tax that reduces holdings before they are bequeathed. Revenues from both these taxes could finance desirable public health care, education, communication, and other programs. In a few years even a 30% wealth tax would hugely reduce disparities in holdings and generate public funds to invest in socially guided programs to rid society of homelessness, hunger, inadequate schools, and other offensive features.

Income taxes

Income due to institutional, organizational, or personal advantages also violates the norm we established last chapter—that is, to remunerate only effort and sacrifice—and is therefore neither moral nor efficient. A way to move toward Just Rewards, therefore, is to demand highly graduated income taxes. This again provides a vehicle to better the lot of those in need in ways that create lasting gains in consciousness and empowerment.

As a last caveat, with all the above tax proposals it is critical that government isn't spending tax revenues on welfare for the rich, giving everything collected back to the wealthiest sectors and undercutting the value of taxing in the first place. Rather the demand for what to do with increased taxes on the wealthy needs to be to rebuild inner cities, enhance public health, improve public education, etc.

Affirmative Action

> *There are really not many jobs that actually*
> *require a penis or a vagina, and all other*
> *occupations should be open to everyone.*
> *-Gloria Steinem*

In addition to people owning capital or monopolizing conditions that enhance bargaining power, racism and sexism can also distort remuneration, bending it away from rewarding only effort and sacrifice by miscounting the effort and sacrifice and the worthiness of particular constituencies.

While the typical white household in the U.S. had $18,000 in financial wealth (net worth minus equity in owner-occupied housing) in 1995, which is the latest year for which complete figures are available at the time of writing, the typical black household had just $200 and the typical Hispanic household had zero. Similarly, in 1991, 39.2 percent of white American households had incomes less than $25,000, but among Hispanics 54.4 percent were below $25,000, and for black Americans 60.6 percent were less than $25,000.

Similarly, women who work outside the home earn only 62% as much as men, which is up from 47% in 1980 and from 38% in 1970. Struggle does pay off, but the situation is still obviously inadequate. Women who work full-time earn three-quarters what men do, up from the three-fifths that prevailed through most of the 1970s.

Likewise, and even more important, despite great advances in the past forty years, people of different races and genders still don't generally get comparable work. Instead, by a variety of mechanisms, not only income for jobs, but also jobs themselves are often allocated on the basis of race or gender. In that sense, the culture and conditions of U.S. employment have for a long time acted as a kind of "affirmative action" for whites and men, providing them bastions of employment more or less blocked off to other constituencies.

Demands that would equalize pay for comparable work, remove barriers to entry to better jobs, and facilitate entry to fields with currently skewed participation will all help reduce race and gender effects on income. Typically advocates of existing relations try to portray affirmative action as seeking to undercut white-only and male-only jobs in ways that divide workers from one another. One obvious solution is to have affirmative action both for overcoming caste oppression (race and gender) and for overcoming class oppression as well. A second solution is to finance affirmative action out of funds redistributed from the top, coupling affirmative action with demands for full employment to ensure that the gains of affirmative action for excluded groups don't result in worsening conditions for white male workers already suffering the impoverishment and indignities of capitalism.

Proper Remuneration

The love of money as a possession—as distinguished from the love of money as a means to the enjoyments and realities of life—will be recognized for what it is, a somewhat disgusting morbidity, one of those semi-criminal, semi-pathological propensities which one hands over with a shudder to the specialists in mental disease.
-John Maynard Keynes

Beneath capitalists and coordinators in modern capitalist economies are normal workers who lack capital, who lack inflated bargaining power due to access to decision-making and skill monopolies, who work without significant say over their conditions, who follow orders given by others, and who are rarely remunerated at an appropriate rate for their effort and sacrifice. Perhaps one out of five adults in the United States fall in the property owning or the skill and decision monopolizing classes. The remaining four fifths are the working class and receive relatively meager income and accumulate minimal wealth despite expending more effort and sacrifice in their work than the elite coordinators and capitalists. The third set of programmatic demands for Just Rewards seeks to raise remuneration for those currently being paid too little for the effort and sacrifice they expend. There are many approaches.

Full employment

Part of the income accruing from various taxes should support government full employment policies that will have the following beneficial results: (1) the unemployed immediately gain employment and income, (2) all workers benefit from increased bargaining power due to reduced fear of being fired, and (3) society benefits from additional output guided by social choice rather than profit-seeking.

Minimum wage supports

Increasing the minimum wage, in conjunction with attaining full employment, puts a floor on personal income. However, minimum wage jobs are almost always the most onerous. Thus, if we were already rewarding only effort and sacrifice, they would be the highest paid in society, not the lowest. Still, a short-run program must move modestly in the right direction before it can gather momentum and finally win magnificent new structures. Thus a demand for a minimum wage that is 60% of the average income for the economy would be a good short-term beginning point. To howls that this would bankrupt many businesses, an answer might be to reduce payroll at higher levels in those businesses or for the government to use accrued profit and property taxes to subsidize worthy smaller operations made "needy" by the program. On the other hand, we should note that operations which cannot pay appropriate wages are in many instances not ones that are socially desirable to maintain, and if we have full employment, their having to close up shop is not a debit of our demands. To make this point stark—suppose that if McDonalds had to pay just wages and provide just conditions (much less cover the health costs its food induces) it couldn't earn profits for its owners. Do we lose if McDonalds is in that manner forced out of business? Well, its owners would certainly lose the profits they were accruing by paying their employees horribly. But the employees, in a full employment economy, would only benefit.

Social wage payments

The "social wage" is a loose term for government policies that benefit working people. This includes expenditures on public health care, education, housing, and infrastructure, or even price supports on essential goods or food stuffs, so as to reduce income demands on the poor. Policies that increase allocations for the "Social Wage" redistribute society's product to benefit those in need, and thus also move society toward Just Rewards.

Reverse income taxes

Just as it is possible to collect taxes, it is also possible to pay reverse taxes. Since our economy doesn't directly remunerate according to effort and sacrifice, the government can "tax and pay" to correct deviations from this norm, not only taking away from those who are over-rewarded, but also paying out to those who are under-rewarded. The ideal demand is for a socially regulated accounting of job types that generates a measure of their broad implications for effort and sacrifice, plus a reverse payment for those that are under-remunerated by the market system. In this manner the funds accrued from profit, wealth, luxury, inheritance, and income taxes can be redistributed not only to social wage payments for public education, health care, etc., but also as reverse taxes paid directly to workers who are earning less than their job requirements warrant. Obviously, even demands well short of optimal would be very progressive in their impact, and the discussion and organization required to bring them about could only be positive.

Job actions for higher wages

Naturally, a program seeking participatory economics will also support union and rank and file efforts to win higher wages by collective bargaining, strikes, etc. This raises incomes that are currently too low. It can also cut into incomes that are currently too high. And this program should foster activism that prepares the organizational means and worker commitment to win still further gains.

Fighting For Just Rewards in a Movement for Participatory Economics

It is not, as has sometimes been said by those indulging in metaphysical woolliness, just a question of giving the worker "the total product of his labor," it is a question of completely reshaping the relationships ... in the factory, in the village, in the store, in production, and in distribution of supplies.
- Peter Kropotkin

One does not sell the ground upon which the people walk.
- Crazy Horse

Finally, a movement that seeks Just Rewards in society has to practice what it preaches. If society ought to have Just Rewards, so should movement work have Just Rewards. This is necessary for the movement: (a) to be believable, (b) to expand its own understanding of what its aims entail, (c) to provide hope through its internal practice, and (d) to welcome and nurture diverse participation. This last point is especially important but rarely enunciated. What underpaid person would believe in the honesty of a movement that talks about attaining Just Rewards in society, but that doesn't practice Just Rewards internally? Thus, in a consistent movement for a participatory economy, its own internal dues (movement taxation) and wage rates should exceed its Just Reward demands for society.

4. Self-Management

*... all authority is quite degrading. It degrades
those who exercise it, and degrades those over
whom it is exercised....When it is used with a
certain amount of kindness, and accompanied
by prizes and rewards, it is dreadfully
demoralizing. People, in that case, are less
conscious of the horrible pressure that is being
put on them, and so go through their lives in a
sort of coarse comfort, like petted animals, without ever
realizing that they are probably thinking other people's
thoughts, living by other people's standards, wearing
practically what one may call other people's secondhand
clothes, and never being themselves for a single moment.*
—Oscar Wilde

Any economy of course involves many decisions, from the
far reaching to the relatively narrow. Who decides? How
much say should each actor in any economy have over decisions in that economy? We believe the answer ought to be that
each actor should have decision-making input proportionate
to the degree he or she is affected by outcomes, or what we call
"self-management." We prefer this to the more typical answers that we ought to favor "economic freedom" or the right
to do whatever one wishes with one's person and property, or
to everyone having equal say over all economic decisions all
the time, or to giving the more knowledgeable or successful
more say than those who are less knowledgeable or less successful. What is the logic of preferring self-management as
our decision-making goal?

Decision Settings

A man may fish with the worm that hath eat of a
king, and eat of the fish that hath fed of that worm.
-Shakespeare

My notion of democracy is that under it the weakest shall
have the same opportunities as the strongest. . .No
country in the world today show any but patronizing
regard for the weak. . . True democracy cannot be
worked by twenty men sitting at the center. It has to
be worked from below, by the people of every village.
- Gandhi

Imagine a worker in a plant has his own work area. Suppose also that he wants to put a picture of his daughter on the wall. How much say should he have? More to the point, how much say should I have about his daughter's picture if I work across the plant in another division, or even across town?

Suppose another worker wants to play Punk Rock or New Age Jazz all day long in her area. How much say over that should she have? And how much say should I have if I work just a little way up the floor from her, well within the "hearing zone?" Or what if I work across town?

Suppose a work team in some workplace is deciding a shared schedule. How much say should each member have relative to the others, or to other workers in the plant? What about folks who use the group's outputs in another part of the plant? What about folks who consume the plant's products across town or on the other side of the country?

Or suppose you live near my plant...what say should you have relative to me about the noise emanating from my plant into your neighborhood? You consume products that I help produce. How much say should you have about what the plant produces, about our choices for organization and output, and about my work situation?

These are all very serious and germane questions. There is no single answer, of course. It can't be that in every one of these cases the person should have full say or no say, equal say or less or more say. The cases differ. It can't be that one-person one-vote majority rule is always optimal, or three fifths, or consensus, and so on. They differ. But perhaps there is at least a single norm that covers all of these cases and all other economic decision-making as well.

Self Management

It is an abuse of words to apply the same term "discipline" to such unrelated concepts as the mindless reflex motions of a body with a thousand hands and a thousand legs, and the spontaneous coordination of the conscious political acts of a group of people. What can the well ordered docility of the former have in common with the aspirations of a class struggling for its emancipation?
-Rosa Luxembourg

Why should workers agree to be slaves in a basically authoritarian structure? They should have control over it themselves. Why shouldn't communities have a dominant voice in running the institutions that affect their lives?
- Noam Chomsky

Clearly, a worker ought to have dictatorial say over the picture of his daughter on her desk. She decides, I have no say from my cubicle next door. But from that next cubicle, I should have a veto over my neighbor worker's option to play punk rock in her area all day. Similarly, a work group should have most say about its operational choices, but groups that consume its product should have some say as well, in proportion to the extent they are affected. Once one takes the time to express these simple points, the obvious lesson is that:

1) Decisions often differ in how much they affect different individuals or constituencies. And,

2) As a result, one-person one-vote majority rule, or two-thirds rule, or consensus, or dictatorship, or any other particular decision-making approach is merely a tactical option for implementing some more general norm in a specific context, rather than an end in itself. But then it also follows that:

3) To enshrine a single decision-making method as always applicable —whether one-person one-vote, or consensus, or dictatorial say for one person—ignores that different approaches to allocating decision-making influence fit different situations, even if we are trying to accomplish the same favored norm.

So what we really need is not to elevate one decision- making method over all others, but to choose our decision-making methods based on how appropriate they are to best accomplish a preferred norm in the specific context we confront.

But what norm should we regularly aspire to? Assuming we respect everyone involved, when we spontaneously decide how to make specific decisions in daily life, we automatically try to give each actor a say proportionate to the degree they are affected. We don't have one friend among many decide on a movie for all to see, nor do we just count up votes. All friends have input, and if someone has seen a movie or has some other pressing need, they may get more say about that. And while we can't always perfectly attain a level of self-management wherein everyone has decision-making input perfectly proportionate to the degree they are affected by outcomes, we intuitively know in our personal lives that any deviation from this means at least one person is having excessive impact while at least one other person is denied their fair share of impact.

Certainly there are sometimes reasons to violate proportionate input for all. Suppose there is a sudden announcement that a tidal wave is heading our way. One of us is a tidal wave survival expert, the rest are city-folk who know nothing about the matter. A quick shift to dictatorship is prudent. But does this insight abrogate our natural inclination to advocate decision-making input in proportion to effect as our guiding norm for a good economy? Does it suggest we ought to instead adopt, as many would advocate, decision-making input in accordance with relevant knowledge and the quality of decisions we might expect a person to arrive at? Let's see.

Knowledge and Decisions

That reorganization will depend, first and foremost, on the thorough familiarity of labor with the economic situation of the country; on a complete inventory of the supply, on exact knowledge of the sources of raw material, and on the proper organization of the labor forces for efficient management.
-Alexander Berkman

Relevant knowledge for decisions comes in two forms.

1) There is knowledge of the character of the decision and its context and of its most likely implications. And

2) There is also knowledge of how each person feels about those implications and specifically how they value the various options.

The first type of knowledge is often quite specialized, as in the case of the tidal wave hero who has a complete monopoly on it. But the second type of knowledge is always dispersed, since we are each individually the world's foremost experts regarding our own personal valuations. I know best that I don't want to drown. I am the world's foremost expert regarding my valuations of situations impacts on me. You are regarding your own. Shawn, Sally, Sue, Sam, and Samantha are regarding their own. Now it may be that Sally is also the world's foremost expert on some situation's likely properties and possibilities...but that is different than how either she or I feel about that situation's likely effects on her or on me.

So whenever the conclusions of specialized knowledge about implications can be disseminated sufficiently that each actor can assess the situation and arrive at their own view of how they are affected in ample time to express it for the decision, each actor should have impact proportionately to the effects they will endure. Whenever that's impossible for some reason and the costs of making a mistake would be high, then we may need to temporarily function according to a different norm that temporarily cedes authority, though in ways that don't permanently subvert our prior self-managing aim. Obviously, the burden of proof is on deviating from what is most desirable, and the implication for needing to distribute knowledge to permit self-management is evident.

In short, the fact that you are a chemist and understand the chemistry and biology of lead paint on walls and what effects it can have, whereas I am a painter or an auto-maker, and do not understand the involved chemistry, but only the implications that you convey, doesn't mean that you get to decide disproportionately whether my walls have lead paint or whether our whole community permits or rejects lead paint. It does mean, however, that my fellow community members and I should listen to your expert testimony before making a decision. You are a valued source, by all means, but in the decision-making per se, you become like everyone else. In promulgating information, you are an expert, but in the decision itself, you have a say proportionate to the effect on you, just as we have a say proportionate to the effect on us.

Councils and Other Implications

Thus council organization weaves a variegated net of collaborating bodies through society, regulating its life and progress according to their own free initiative. And all that in the councils is discussed and decided draws its actual power from the understanding, the will, the action of working humankind itself.
-Anton Pannekoek

*Listen, Revolution, We're buddies, see—Together, We can
take everything: Factories, arsenals, houses, ships, Railroads,
forests, fields, orchards, Bus lines, telegraphs, radios,
(Jesus! Raise hell with radios!) Steel mills, coal mines,
oil wells, gas, All the tools of production, (Great day in the
morning!) Everything—And turn 'em over to the people
who work. Rule and run 'em for us people who work.*

- *Langston Hughes*

So the self-management goal is that each actor influences decisions in proportion as he or she is affected, any deviation being understood to give some actors too much say and others
too little. To achieve self-management and have the decisions
be good ones, each actor must have easy access to relevant assessments of anticipated outcomes, and must have sufficient
general knowledge and intellectual confidence to understand
the assessments and develop preferences in light of them. Society's organization should insure that sources of analysis related to decision making are unbiased, diverse, and well
tested. Thus for self-management, each individual or group
involved in a decision must have organizational means to arrive at and make known their desires, as well as the means to
tally them sensibly, with their well-informed input having the
proper proportionate influence.

In an economy, to achieve this informed self-management,
we need various institutions (which we call different sized
workers' and consumers' councils) to serve as decision-making
vehicles for different size collectives of workers and consumers. Thus, work-group, division, workplace, industry, and living group, neighborhood, community, and county councils are
needed as vehicles for those affected by decisions to express
individual and group preferences about those decisions, voting their preferences, implementing results, etc. We also need
information dispersal that provides the knowledge necessary
for informed judgments about economic interactions by all
those affected by them. It's also necessary that each actor has
personal confidence and is sufficiently empowered that they
feel comfortable arriving at, expressing, arguing on behalf of,

and voting for their preferences. And finally we need means of allocation, workplace organization, and other institutional interactions that respect and promote the self-management norm and fulfill the requirements of open information dispersal and worker empowerment.

There are many institutional implications of striving for decision-making influence in proportion to the extent one is affected, and discerning even the major implications of this norm takes some doing. But the norm itself is straightforward. Next chapter we offer a program of demands and actions aimed at fostering economic self-management. Further chapters address additional features that bear on this aim, such as workplace organization and how allocation occurs.

5. Q&A: Self Management

Authority tends to make its possessor unjust and
arbitrary; it also makes those subject to it
acquiesce in wrong, subservient, and servile.
Authority corrupts its holder and debases its victim.
-Mikhail Bakunin

• *Would a parecon squelch dissent? It worries me that a*
Chomsky equivalent (although let's hope that s/he would
have one hell of a lot less to say...) might find it even more
difficult to speak out under parecon than they do under
markets.

I can't see any reason why this would be so. First, no one has
significantly greater resources than anyone else, so a free
press in a parecon is not hobbled by being owned by and
servicing a few. Second, a parecon values diversity. This has
considerable bearing. It means that dissent is valued in its
own right, even in lieu of evidence of its validity, for the proper
reason that progress often depends on it. A society with a
participatory economy would, therefore, I should think, set
aside space and resources to actively support dissent.

• *But wouldn't the community get to decide whether the*
work of a dissenter was worth remunerating?

Parecon does not work like this. The whole community
doesn't pass judgment on each workplace in such a manner.
Rather, a group of people can decide to create a workplace, like
a magazine or whatever, and begin to operate within the economy. Your problem takes the form of whether the output of the

effort has sufficient value to warrant inputs into it. But that isn't just a big vote by everyone...it depends on the folks who want the output. And to prevent undesirable outcomes, society could collectively decide—I believe it would do so, in fact—that minority and dissident viewpoints deserve greatly disproportionate support, beyond what economic accounting might spontaneously arrive at, on the off chance, for example, that they are valid, and will grow in relevance and impact.

- *Couldn't a parecon block dissent in the same way that markets do, perhaps even to the extent that something like your own Z Magazine couldn't exist?*

There is a sense of this, yes. Suppose a few folks decide to create a magazine in a parecon. And suppose very few folks want it—too few, using the typical planning procedures to decide the issue—to warrant the planning system providing us all the inputs we need. What is the option, then?

- Well, we could do it on a volunteer labor basis—trying to get it to catch an audience, and then proceed thereafter.

- Or we could appeal to some bureau for special dispensation, on grounds of the dissident value of the thing—"dissident value" being something the economy recognizes in the large, as a kind of social investment (more or less like philanthropy now, in some senses, but democratically controlled)

So while these are real problems in any society, it is hard for me to see how parecon isn't vastly superior on these axes than any other economic model we know about.

- *For decisions, why not consensus all the time?*

For the same reason we would opt against majority rule all the time, or against each person does whatever they will, anytime—because consensus conveys a particular apportionment of influence that is consistent with the guiding norms in some cases, but not in others.

But I should clarify something. When folks talk about consensus they often conflate two parts—first, communicating clearly and fully, providing room for those affected to express themselves, etc. The process part. Second, each person having a veto over any proposed plan or decision. The decision input part.

The first aspect, the process part, is almost always appropriate and can be appended to any voting arrangement, though this is unlikely in an elitist context. The second aspect, the decision input rights, is the part that sometimes makes sense, but often not, and which a parecon would therefore employ sometimes, but not many other times.

- *But shouldn't everyone agree with each decision?*

No, there is no reason to think that humans, even in the best society we can imagine, will always see eye to eye about everything. Instead, we can predict with perfect confidence that there will be countless situations in which involved, affected parties have conflicting opinions—both values and assessments—that lead them to favor different options. To have strong dissent is not a sign of failure, not at all, and is often essential to vitality and progress, in fact. Now one can ask, what do you do with on-going dissent—and, for example, one very good thing to do, when possible, is to provide a means for its expression in on-going experimentation and exploration so that, among other things, if the "winning" approach proves undesirable, the dissenting one is still on the table for implementation. This is the logic of diversity applied to decisions.

- *Why can't we say "anything goes"? Why can't each party just do their thing? Why must there be constraints on the individual, and if there are, and if the individual violates them, then what? Repression?*

"Anything goes" isn't an option because it is internally inconsistent. If I do whatever I want it can restrict your being able to do whatever you want. So, for example, suppose I want to own you and dispose over your life. You then have no options though I enjoy "anything goes." At a lesser level, suppose I want to employ you as a wage slave—you now have limited options, while I enjoy "anything goes." Both slave owners and capitalists appeal to the idea that they should be free to pursue their agendas, so that defending slavery and wage slavery as their right. The reason this isn't compelling, or shouldn't be, is because their agendas do not leave others with the same freedoms they claim for themselves. Now at a much lesser level, but still relevant, if I want a boom box and you want quiet, we can't both have our way in neighboring work place cubicles. So, there are limits. A good economy, or society, is not organized around the goal "anything goes." Instead, it needs mechanisms by which people can freely choose in context of the free choices of others, and for the economy, that is what parecon provides.

You also ask, if one violates the limits a parecon imposes, what happens? Many possibilities. Folks who are upset may back off from confronting the violation because it just isn't worth their time to make a fuss. Or, if the violation is substantial, there may be intervention—it could be local or it could involve people trained for the task. Having a good society doesn't mean not having disputes, not needing adjudication, not needing intervention to deal humanely but effectively with anti-social folks, much less with serial killers ... but these are matters for the polity, not the economy, save insofar as, if such roles exist in a good economy, remuneration will be for effort and sacrifice, job complexes will be balanced, decision inputs will be proportionate, etc.

6. Seeking Self Management

Once upon a time there was a magnet, and in its close neighborhood lived some steel filings. One day two or three filings felt a sudden desire to go and visit the magnet, and they began to talk of what a pleasant thing it would be to do. Other filings nearby overheard their conversation, and they, too, became infected with the same desire. Still others joined them, till at last all the filings began to discuss the matter, and more and more their vague desire grew into an impulse. "Why not go today?" said some of them; but others were of the opinion that it would be better to wait until tomorrow. Meanwhile, without their having noticed it, they had been involuntarily moving nearer to the magnet, which lay there quite still, apparently taking no heed of them. And so they went on discussing, all the time insensibly drawing nearer to their neighbor; and the more they talked, the more they felt the impulse growing stronger, till the more impatient ones declared that they would go that day, whatever the rest did. Some were heard to say that it was their duty to visit the magnet, and that they ought to have gone long ago. And, while they talked, they moved always nearer and nearer, without realizing they had moved. Then, at last, the impatient ones prevailed, and, with one irresistible impulse, the whole body cried out, "There is no use waiting. We will go today. We will go now. We will go at once." And then in one unanimous mass they swept along, and in another moment were clinging fast to the magnet on every side. Then the magnet smiled—for the steel filings had no doubt at all but that they were paying that visit on their own free will.
                                                                -Oscar Wilde

Agreeing that self-management, or decision-making input in proportion as one is affected, is a core goal for a participatory economic movement, what demands can we fight for today that will help move us toward self-management tomorrow?

Create workers' and consumers' councils

> *If the workers took a notion they could stop all speeding trains; every ship upon the ocean they can tie with mighty chains. Every wheel in the creation every mine and every mill; fleets and armies of the nation, will at their command stand still.*
> *-Joe Hill*

> *I do my work because I cannot look on and see wrong without a protest. I could no more help crying out than I could if I were drowning.*
> *-Emma Goldman*

For each worker in some workplace or industry or each consumer in a neighborhood or county to have a private opinion isolated from her workmates or neighbors will accomplish relatively little. Instead, to make joint decisions and seek new relations, workers and consumers need to meet together to hash out their views, arrive at collective desires, and together advocate preferred options.

Democratic councils are local institutions that workers and consumers use to pursue collective agendas. As a first step to creating worker and consumer councils, meeting to discuss the council idea is a good place to start. Moving on from there to formalize council rules and agree on a local program for council members to pursue lays a foundation for workers and consumers to seek changes regarding everything from wages and conditions to budgets and investments. From here they can refine their agendas in accord with their on-going experiences and their growth in size and strength.

Democratize information access

*Good sense is of all things in the world most equally
distributed, for everybody thinks he is so well supplied with
it, that even those most difficult to please in all other
matters never desire more of it than they already possess.*
-Rene Descartes

*It is not enough that the forms of government should have the
passive or "implied" consent of the governed, but that the
Society will be in health only if it is in the full sense
democratic and self-governing, which implies not only that
all the citizen should have a `right' to influence its policy if
they so desire, but that the greatest possible opportunity
should be afforded for every citizen actually to exercise this
right.*
- G.D.H Cole

No one can make good decisions without accurate and comprehensive information. If you have a right to vote, but you
lack information bearing on your options, the vote becomes a
charade. To participate intelligently, people need information
about the decisions that affect them. Efforts to "open the
books" in workplaces and regarding city, county, state, and
national budgets promote self-management by making information available, a condition central to self-management.
More, demanding that the information be packaged in readily
available and comprehensible ways, and the right to access it
during paid work-time rather than at leisure, also furthers
self-management.

Democratize workplace decision-making

*When the workers are society they will regulate their
labor, so that the supply and demand shall be genuine,
not gambling; the two will then be commensurate,
for it is the same society which demands that*

also supplies; there will be no more artificial
famines, no more poverty amidst over production,
amidst too great a stock of the very things which
should supply poverty and turn it into well being.
In short there will be no waste and therefore no tyranny.
                                        -William Morris

Having councils with informed members creates the possibility to struggle for gains around wages, conditions, prices, investments, and all of economic life. But why should workers and consumers struggle anew for their desires each time a new issue arises? What about winning the right to impact decisions directly, rather than only by virtue of a long, debilitating struggle?

It is good for workers' councils (or unions) to mount a campaign to coerce decision-makers to raise wages and improve conditions, of course. And it is similarly good for consumers' councils or movements to coerce government to alter its budget allotments and enact pollution controls, for example. But it would also be good for either workers' or consumers' councils to meet as part of their members' normal daily responsibilities and calmly raise wages, improve conditions, or alter budgets by virtue of their authorized power in decision-making, without having to fight about it.

In other words, in addition to winning gains via council and union struggles that press for desired results, democratizing economic decision-making also requires winning sanctioned power for councils in the actual decision-making process itself. This power can range from the modest gain of having a council representative or two at industry or government meetings for reporting purposes, to winning some voting rights at such meetings, to winning full empowerment over and above any other sectors of the workplace or government regarding economic decisions.

In short, we use councils and other means at our disposal to fight over conditions and other reforms, of course, but we also fight over the nature of the contest itself, over the rules of conflict and future decision making.

Increase consumers' power over production

*People's lives are in turmoil. There is a sense of crisis for
men as well as for women, and for children too. Do we
have an idea or even a glimmering about how people
can and should live, not as victims as in the past for
women, nor as atoms just whirling around on their own
trajectories, but as moral agents in a human community?*
-Barbara Ehrenreich

What a workplace produces and whether it uses one or another technology should not be entirely decided by folks inside that workplace, even workers' councils. Such decisions also affect the workplace's consumers and neighbors, and the consumers and neighbors should have a say as well.

To incorporate all actors proportionately in decision- making requires increasing the power of those under-represented. Demands for neighborhood oversight committees regarding the ecological and other local impacts of a workplace are desirable, as are demands for consumer say over workplace decisions about products and prices. Such demands can benefit those in need and also expand consciousness, strengthen commitment, and develop new organization for winning still more gains in the future.

Democratize social budgets

*Suppose humans happen to be so constructed that
they desire the opportunity for freely undertaken
productive work. Suppose they want to be free
from the meddling of technocrats and commissars, bankers
and tycoons, mad bombers who engage in psychological
tests of will with peasants defending their homes,
behavioral scientists who can't tell a pigeon from a
poet, or anyone else who tries to wish freedom
and dignity out of existence or beat them into oblivion.*
—Noam Chomsky

Think of a city deciding on its budget for education, sanitation, new housing, a new health clinic, snow removal, or anything else. Who is affected? Most often, all citizens, of course. Who makes the decision? Most often, elite elected officials pressured by local and national corporations trying to maximize profit, of course.

To move toward more participation, progressive demands over the size or purpose of budget items such as national military expenditures, state welfare programs, or local county payments toward a new hospital are certainly good. But demands that make budgets public and that incorporate workers' and consumers' councils into budget decision-making as a natural part of the process are excellent, too.

Indeed, as with every component of a participatory economic program, the overarching idea is that demands that improve conditions for oppressed constituencies are good. But beyond that, if the rhetoric and process of campaigns to win such demands also increases participatory economic solidarity, understanding, and organization, that's an additional important improvement. And finally, if the campaigns can win not only better conditions, but a new playing field on which it is easier to win still more gains in the future, that's ideal.

Institute self-management in our own projects and movements

> ...the only one capable of playing the part of director
> is the collective ego of the working class which has
> sovereign right to make mistakes and to learn
> the dialectics of history by itself. Let us put it
> quite bluntly: the errors committed by a truly revolutionary
> workers' movement are historically far more fruitful
> than the correct decisions of the finest Central Committee.
> -Rosa Luxembourg

> You have to be the change you want to see in the world.
> —Gandhi

Imagine we have a movement that argues forcefully and uncompromisingly that actors should impact economic decisions throughout the whole economy in proportion as they are affected by those decisions. Now imagine that in its own operations this same movement elevates a fund raiser, a big donor, or someone with a lot of training of one sort or another to a position of power over a large staff or even over a vast rank and file membership, removing most participants from proportionate influence or even from any influence at all over the movement's agenda.

This is not a pretty picture. This movement wouldn't learn from and become educated by its own self-managing experience, because it wouldn't actually have a self-managing experience. This movement wouldn't serve as a model legitimating the efficacy of its demands, because it would function instead like the institutions it opposed. This movement wouldn't have a new practice embodying what it preaches, but would instead have an old-fashioned practice undermining its credibility to those it addressed. This movement wouldn't be congenial and empowering for all its members nor welcome their fullest talents and participation, but would instead breed internal strife and bad morale.

For these reasons, structuring itself to incorporate steadily more self-management in its own operations should be a very critical programmatic component of a participatory economic movement. Movement projects headed by a few but staffed by many that do nothing to democratize themselves are poor vehicles for seeking self-management in the broader society they inhabit.

7. Dignified Work

The understandings of the greater part of men are necessarily formed by their ordinary employments ... the man whose life is spent in performing a few simple operations, of which the effects too are, perhaps, always the same, or very nearly the same, has no occasion to exert his understanding ... And generally becomes as stupid and ignorant as it is possible for a human creature to be ... But in every improved and civilized society this is the state into which the laboring poor, that is, the great body of people, must necessarily fall, unless government takes pains to prevent it.
-Adam Smith

Our third thematic goal (after Just Rewards and Self-Management) is about what we call Dignified Work and in particular Balanced Job Complexes. Attaining Dignified Work has two primary components:

1) Attaining a just division of tasks for each person; and

2) Attaining a division of tasks so that our work fosters self-management.

Just Work

I were better to be eaten to death with rust than to be scoured to nothing with perpetual motion.
-Shakespeare

A just division of tasks requires that each person should have a fair share of good and bad quality of life attributes in their workday or, if they don't, that they be remunerated accordingly. In other words, why should one person have nice work conditions and another person horrible ones, unless the latter person is given extra pay to offset his or her burden?

But conveniently for us, this element of Just Work is already accomplished in our unfolding participatory economic vision because remunerating according to effort and sacrifice, as per our earlier chapters, automatically offsets any disparity in quality of life attributes. That is, if we remunerate according to effort and sacrifice, whenever Betty works at a less fulfilling and more demanding job than Salim, Betty will also exert more effort and sacrifice at work and will therefore get appropriately higher pay than Salim. So we already have Just Work due to our prior agreements about Just Rewards. But is that all there is to attaining Dignified Work?

Equally Empowering Work

That which we at present call laziness is, rather, the disgust which men [sic] feel over breaking their backs for beggars' salaries and being, moreover, looked down upon and depreciated by the class which exploits them—while those who do nothing useful live like princes and are deferred to and respected by all.
-Ricardo Flores Magon

We also want our economic actors to influence outcomes in proportion as they are affected by them: self-management. Suppose Betty spends all day cleaning floors and Salim spends all day doing empowering financial and social tasks that increase his decision-making related skills and knowledge. Even if Betty and Salim have the same workplace voting rights and even if they are remunerated justly, after months of working at these differently empowering jobs, Betty will have neither the energy, knowledge, confidence, nor skills to play a role comparable to Salim's in influencing decisions.

Workplace council meetings involve discussion, presentation, debate, and votes. If Salim comes to meetings with extensive knowledge, social skills, confidence, and energy due to his empowering job and Betty comes to the same meetings with depleted knowledge, social skills, confidence, and energy due to her dis-empowering job, Salim will have much more impact at the meetings than Betty. In fact, the relatively few workers with highly empowering jobs will, by virtue of their on-the-job situations, dominate discussions. Even a fair vote will regularly select among proposals that only the empowered few offer, and settle on proposals that they collectively come to favor. At best Betty will ratify the will of the empowered, informed, and energetic few. At worst, she and everyone else with a disempowering job will be entirely excluded.

It follows that attaining Self-Management requires not only the formal right to participate in decisions, but also that everyone enjoys conditions that prepare and promote their effective participation. If an economy is class-divided so that those with empowering jobs make decisions that others obey and those with disempowering jobs merely obey decisions that others make, there will not be self-management, clearly. So if workers are to participate equally in decision-making, their diverse jobs must affect their decision-making inclinations and competence comparably. The old slogan that you are what you eat may or may not be economically meaningful. But the new slogan that you become what you do, is surely economically pivotal. This is why we highlight Dignified Work as a key liberatory theme unto itself.

Balanced Job Complexes

I refuse to accept the idea that the 'isness' of man's
present nature makes him morally incapable of
reaching up for the 'oughtness' that forever confronts him.
-Martin Luther King, Jr

In any economy, each job combines many tasks which, taken in combination, have an overall "empowerment index." This index is higher if the sum total of tasks in the job are more empowering, and lower if they are less empowering. Jobs in typical corporations combine quite similar tasks into such jobs as secretary, mail boy, janitor, CEO, finance officer, assembly line operator, manager, and so on. Most people in these corporations do jobs that have a low empowerment index. A very few do jobs that have a very high index.

To attain Balanced Job Complexes, we instead advocate apportioning tasks to jobs so that each job in the economy has an average overall index. In other words, we allot to each job not a homogenous batch of tasks at only one empowerment level, but a combination of tasks with varied empowerment qualities whose total empowerment effect is the average for society. Instead of Judy being a secretary, John being a comptroller, and Jerry cleaning bathrooms, Judy, John, and Jerry all have a variety of tasks in their designated job with various levels of rote and empowering implications. The overall empowerment effect on Judy of her combination of tasks and on John of his and on Jerry of his, are, as best we can manage it, the same.

In other words, with balanced job complexes we of course each have a job in which we enjoy our own particular and perhaps even unique conditions of work. However, despite considerable differences in specific content from what others do, our job and all other jobs are comparably empowering.

As a result of balancing job complexes there is no longer a fixed management with uniquely informative and uplifting tasks. There is no longer a set of rote jobs whose conditions are only deadening. Indeed, there is no hierarchy of jobs vis-à-vis empowerment effects at all. We define all this hierarchy away by combining tasks into jobs in this new way, balancing tasks for empowerment effects. Thus, each person working in the economy does a combination of tasks sensibly accommodated to the needs of particular work situations, but also designed to balance empowerment rather than to monopolize the most empowering circumstances for a few folks at the top of a work-place hierarchy.

Okay, it is clear that by its very definition balancing job complexes accomplishes a greater degree of fairness and also lays a proper foundation for self-management. It avoids dividing the workforce into a highly-empowered "coordinator class" and a subordinate, disenfranchised working class, instead giving all workers comparable empowerment in their economic lives. But are there offsetting problems with the approach? For example, can it get the work done, and can it get it done well?

Individual Options

So you see, I claim that work in a duly ordered community
should be made attractive by the consciousness of usefulness,
by its being carried on with intelligent interest, by variety,
and by its being exercised amidst pleasurable surroundings.
-William Morris

Folks at largely rote jobs will generally like the idea of balanced job complexes because their lives will improve as they receive their fair share of empowering tasks in their work. They will therefore see the switch from unbalanced to balanced jobs as justly redressing a demeaning and unfair situation they have long suffered.

On the other hand, folks who occupy or who aspire to have cushier and more empowered jobs such as managers, doctors, lawyers, empowered intellectuals, etc., will often see this proposal as threatening because after job complexes are newly balanced, their old jobs would no longer exist in the same form as they held them earlier. A person in an economy with balanced job complexes may certainly do some managing (of a sort), doctoring, lawyering, conducting, researching, designing, composing, etc., but this person would also have to do a fair share of less empowering tasks to attain an overall balance like everyone else's. Thus, people's jobs who are now in relatively commanding positions will lose some empowering tasks and incorporate a fair share of less empowering, rote, or even deadening labor.

In any event, whoever enunciates it, opposition to job balancing most often employs one of two rationales:

1. Balancing would impinge my freedom to do what I want, which would be immoral.

2. Balancing would consign even the most talented to rote tasks and thereby reduce the social product to everyone's disadvantage.

Let's consider each complaint in turn, to close out our case on behalf of Dignified Work.

Freedom

> *Freedom is not merely the opportunity to do as one pleases; neither is it merely the opportunity to choose between set alternatives. Freedom is, first of all, the chance to formulate the available choices, to argue over them—and then, the opportunity to choose.*
> —*C. Wright Mills.*

It is true that allowing only balanced job complexes would by definition preclude anyone having an unbalanced job complex and would thus also preclude complainant 1 above from doing only empowering tasks as her job. However, this is true in the same sense that reshaping an economy to have no slave- holding options precludes anyone from owning slaves. That is, owning a slave means the slave-owner freely expresses his slave-owning aspiration, but it also means that someone else is owned. If we rule out that anyone should be owned, we simultaneously rule out that slave-owning aspirations should be honored. Similarly, having a job complex that is more empowering than average is only possible at the expense of someone else having a job complex that is less empowering than average. If we rule out that anyone should be saddled with a less than average complex, yes, we must also rule out that anyone can have a more than average complex.

Freedom to act on one's aspirations is a valid and wonderful thing only so long as it is contingent on everyone else having the same freedom. Some aspirations—owning slaves, killing a neighbor, employing wage slaves, having an unbalanced job complex—intrinsically impinge on others' rights to similar advantages. In other words, it is no more immoral to impose job balancing on society to eliminate a class hierarchy of those who order and those who obey, than it is to impose abolition of slavery on society in order to eliminate a class hierarchy of those who own others and those who are owned by others. All people's rights to never be a slave trump Mr. Plantation's right to own slaves. Similarly, all people's rights to enjoy conditions prerequisite to self-management trump Ms. Manager's right to monopolize empowering job circumstances.

Productivity

> *The difference of natural talents in different men*
> *is, in reality, much less than we are aware of;*
> *and the very different genius which appears*
> *to distinguish men of different professions, when*
> *grown up to maturity, is not upon many occasions*
> *so much the cause, as the effect of the division of labour.*
> *- Adam Smith*

What about output? Seeking to avoid a class division between order-givers and order-takers, are we also reducing society's overall productivity by under-utilizing some folks' capacities? If so, is the loss in output so great that it makes balancing job complexes unwise?

I should first clarify that even if job balancing would in fact sacrifice some output, it wouldn't cause me to renounce Dignified Work as a goal since I see self-management and classlessness as far more worthy aspirations than attaining maximum output. In fact, however, it turns out that we can cook our cake with dignity and eat plenty of it too.

First, normal human beings generally don't work endless hours at empowering and productive tasks. Rather, folks with a relative monopoly on empowering tasks often do them some limited amount of time each week, spending a lot of other time chatting, loafing, meeting, bossing other people around, or playing golf. Realignment of their responsibilities so they are balanced could be done without much incursion on their most productive capabilities. Instead we could replace their excessive time off or their time bossing others with more rote responsibilities.

But second, suppose I'm wrong. Suppose that every hour that someone now doing highly empowering tasks is asked to do more rote tasks is an hour subtracted from time going to their most talented focus. As complainant 2 fears, that would certainly entail a loss in output from that person. For example, if a surgeon who now works all day long on surgery (no desk work, no loafing, no golf) suddenly has to do her share of less empowering work such as cleaning bed pans, then to make room she must of course do less surgery, and she will in total therefore generate less valuable output.

But what about the other side of the coin? What about the nurse who in this new context is better trained and able to more fully use her talents? Indeed, how about all the people previously "dumbed-down" by schooling and then by on-the-job boredom, and who have been previously constrained to do only rote tasks but now have Dignified Work to do? What about the creativity, talent, and skills that would be newly-tapped for society due to 80% of the population now being socialized and schooled to fulfill their capabilities rather than channeled as before into rote obedience and subservience? Does anyone really believe that the sum total of creative talents and energies available for production would be reduced by opting for an economic arrangement that enjoins every actor to become as able and productive as they can be, and that provides the means for them to do it, but that then also requires each to do a fair share of non-empowering work as well as a fair share of what their talents are best suited to?

If current class-divided societies were perfect meritocracies in the sense of welcoming every person to become as productive as possible, and then rewarding with better work conditions and more empowering circumstances only those who produce more so that any effort to balance circumstances among workers would reduce output, then we should still overwhelmingly favor balanced job complexes. Our guiding value should not be the size of output of an economy—but instead equitably meeting needs and developing capacities while furthering values we aspire to such as self-management, solidarity, equity, and diversity. But in reality, societies with hierarchical distributions of tasks don't even remotely approach being perfect meritocracies. Instead, in such societies, an educated and credentialed elite monopolizes empowering and knowledge-enhancing tasks partly due to their talents, yes, but overwhelmingly due to their circumstantial advantages and their willingness to trample those below. Without job balancing, that is, most members of an economy are propelled into relative subservience not by a lack of potential, but by degrading and disempowering socialization, schooling, and on-the-job circumstances. They could instead certainly partake in decision-making and creative work, given the opportunity to express their capacities and enjoy a balanced job complex. The gains from these changes would be enormous.

The second complainant also fails to notice the amount of time, energy, and talent that goes into maintaining the exploitative exclusion of most actors from empowering work and into coercing their obedience to instructions that they are alienated from. If we account for the difference between class-divided workplaces and dignified workplaces regarding time given to oversight and enforcement and time lost due to outright struggle and strife, and if we also account for the new pools of talent salvaged by utilizing previously squelched potentials, not only does the switch to balanced job complexes from hierarchical ones emerge as preferable on moral grounds and on grounds of laying a basis for real self-management, but also on grounds of economic output.

Indeed, the only drawback for balancing job complexes, at least viewed from the angle of those now enjoying a relative monopoly on empowering work, is that it removes their relative advantages. But that is precisely the purpose of job balancing, at least when viewed from below—and that's where our eyes ought to be seeing from.

8. Q&A: Dignified Work

Now, as to occupations, we shall clearly not be able to have the same division of labor in [our workplaces] as now: vicarious servanting, sewer-emptying, butchering, letter carrying, boot-blacking, hair -dressing, and the rest of it, will have come to an end; we shall either make all these occupations agreeable to ourselves in some mood... or we shall have to let them lapse altogether. A great many fidgety occupations will come to an end: we shan't put a pattern on a cloth or a twiddle on a jug-handle to sell it, but to make it prettier and to amuse ourselves and others.
-William Morris

* *Parecon is hard to explain quickly to my friends. Can you cram it into one sentence?*

In a participatory economy (1) remuneration is according to effort and sacrifice, (2) jobs are balanced for empowerment and desirability, and (3) democratic councils of workers and consumers propose and revise what work and consumption they will do until other workers and consumers agree that the proposals are equitable and make efficient use of society's resources—through "participatory planning."

* *What exactly is a balanced job complex?*

A balanced job complex is a collection of tasks within a workplace comparable in its burdens and benefits, and in its impact on the worker's ability to participate in decision- making, to all other job complexes in that workplace and across the economy. Workers have responsibility for a job complex in their main workplace, and often for additional tasks outside to balance their overall work responsibilities with those of other workers in society.

- *Why don't we forgo the balanced job complexes and just have jobs structured like now but paid according to effort and sacrifice?*

Parecon opts for balanced job complexes to promote equity of circumstances, yes, but also because balanced job complexes are an essential choice if we want actors to be prepared and able to participate in the decisions that affect them.

It would be materially and socially just regarding the allocation of tasks and rewards to do as you say. If someone has an odious and deadening job, and another person has a delightful and enriching one, pay the former person more than the latter—in accord with effort and sacrifice. But if we ignore the empowerment effects of workplace roles we will permit a class division between coordinators (monopolizing tasks that impart power and knowledge) and workers (delegated tasks that disempower), which division would in time yield a redefinition of norms of remuneration until the coordinators had both the desirable work and the higher incomes.

Also, even in lieu of this large-scale effect, if you don't balance for empowerment you can't have participatory self-management because different sectors of people are differentially able to use formally democratic means of influencing outcomes. Think of a bunch of people sitting around to make a decision with equal formal say—but suppose some of them have circumstances that give them required knowledge and skills relevant to decision making, and others are just exhausted and deadened by their circumstances with no time to assess options or develop agendas. The latter folks are left choosing among options that the former folks advocate, on the basis of arguments the former folks offer...at best. This is the heart of the logic of balanced job complexes: full justice needs job complexes balanced for empowerment plus remuneration according to effort and sacrifice. You can also have balance for quality of life effects (which will equalize wages for equal hours at a balanced job complex) or not, in this analysis.

- *Wouldn't balanced job complexes be unfair for highly trained people? There are quite a few 'upper-level' jobs that require years of schooling that actually are really boring and somewhat unpleasant.*

Two issues. Years of schooling. And boring. Schooling, like working, is part of one's complex assuming it is socially beneficial, once one is beyond the basic graduation age. So that is no problem. If schooling were horribly onerous, it would be remunerated accordingly, but of course that is generally nonsense as schooling is generally much less onerous (and certainly would be in a good society) than the less desirable work tasks that need doing. Give anyone the option of going to grad school for living wages, for example, or working the same period in a coal mine for—double, triple, or even five times as much—and their choice is pretty obvious. But, however society turns out to assess these options, so it goes. As to boring and onerous and dangerous, those attributes are remunerated more highly due to requiring more effort and sacrifice.

- *If you removed the money, prestige, and opportunity to boss around underlings from jobs, why would anyone waste their youth studying to become an industrial waste engineer when they could study art or hop trains around the country instead?*

In a parecon, if these types of work (altered as they would be in such an economy) are horribly onerous, fewer people will be doing them because there will be much less demand for the high priced output. I would have preferred when I was a student, to develop my mathematical and scientific talents, not something for which I have no talent. And I think this is rather typical—that is, that people would usually (not always) like to do what they are good at, assuming that in later life they could make use of that learning, etc. Another factor is what you can get to do, and its worth to you, later. This can be a quality of life assessment, a service to the community assessment, or an income assessment (in economies other than parecons, anyhow).

In making one's choice in a parecon, there is no way to make a financial killing. And if you would prefer to develop fewer of your talents, or develop them less fully, so it goes. There is nothing to prevent it.

As to now, I would wager that there isn't a coordinator class person around who would switch to an assembly line job, say, even if offered a higher wage than their current one. Not one. But please consider, what makes more empowered jobs boring and rote and unrewarding, to the extent they are? Isn't it in large part their still limited say (capitalists still rule, not them) and on the other hand the pains associated with the power over others that they have, as well as the often inane character of the things they produce for another's profit? All this changes in a parecon, of course.

So I believe that you are right that a great many people occupying what I call coordinator class jobs are currently horribly distraught at their circumstances and activities—for example, think of high paid and self-governing art directors who produce idiotic ads. But I think they also recognize that compared to folks with rote jobs, less status, and even less power, they are quite privileged.

The main thing is that the causes of the alienated character of work at every level, disappear in parecon. Some things are still onerous, of course, but nothing is alienated, nor is there unfair remuneration. In this context, people will utilize their skills and capacities because it is fulfilling of their natures to do so and because there is pleasure to be had in contributing at a higher level to the social product (by choosing to work where one has most ability); but you are right that they won't earn more for doing it.

- *Wouldn't it be horribly inefficient for doctors and other highly trained professionals to be required to do unskilled work like changing bedpans?*

It depends, as always, what you mean by efficiency. For
Mozart to do unskilled work instead of writing music costs humanity every time it occurs far more than for me to do unskilled work rather than, oh, whatever I may do that is skilled.
This is true enough, due to his amazing genius and its irreplaceable productivity. And that could be true for some excep-
tional surgeon, too, I guess.

The question is what happens when we talk in terms of
large numbers of people, and also what is at stake beyond
merely the material or service product of each person's labors.
Thus, for whatever losses society incurs for some people
spending some time not utilizing their greatest and most re-
vered talents—even in the case of geniuses—how much is
gained by the release of new talents and genius from constituencies previously dumbed-down to fit rote work slots? More,
how much is gained, in a social sense, from attaining equity of
circumstances and empowerment? It is pointless to look at one
side of a trade-off without attending to the other side.

In parecon, the point is that each actor occupies a balanced
job complex of his or her or choosing, from among all those
available that he or she is qualified for. To prepare for this balance, each actor's education needs to leave them capable of informed and effective participation in decision-making. As
well, the economy can only benefit from all actors using, as
they choose, their educational experience to enlarge their potentials and capacities, and from the education system promoting this result for everyone. This is quite the opposite from
now. In capitalism, by contrast, the economy needs workers
made suitable to the available job offerings (this much is always true, in any economy) and since capitalist offerings are
highly skewed, requiring that most actors are accustomed to
boredom, have no expectations of controlling their circumstances, have no related skills or knowledge, and so on, school
must dumb them down. In other words, the economy needs
the school system to dumb people down in order that they can
be shoe-horned into its limited role offerings. In parecon precisely the opposite obtains. People are fully educated, and the
role offerings continually alter in accord.

So, even if we ignore the increases in justice and sociality gained from having balanced job complexes—the question over output becomes do we lose more by the fact that Mozart and some great surgeon have to spend time on tasks that are onerous or boring than we gain by the fact that (a) there are many more Mozarts and people of great surgical talents discovered due to a school system and culture that promotes excellence in all its citizens, and (b) across the board we are getting more capacity-enrichment and utilization from everyone who was previously dumbed-down and consigned to have their talents hidden and made dormant if not killed altogether?

- *If everyone did what they love to do, rather than what they love plus a few unpleasant duties, would the "goods and services produced" be sufficient to provide a decent, sustainable living for everyone?*

This is not the right question. The answer is no, quite obviously, they wouldn't be available; but still it is not the right question. Why wouldn't enough output be available? Because no one would choose to do onerous and debilitating tasks if told, for example, these are not necessary, they don't have to be done, there is no reason or need for you to worry about their being done—the only reason for you to even think about doing them is if they happen to fit your personal, singular, desires so that you would enjoy doing them even if the outputs were redundant.

Now in reality, mature and thinking folks would apportion themselves to those tasks, I think, rather than seeing everyone suffer. But that is unfair because in that case the childish and/or anti-social deadbeats get a better existence for no morally justifiable reason. And there is another problem, as well, even if everyone is trying to be responsible. Suppose, that is, that everyone is mature and thinking—not deadbeat. How do they manage to apportion the onerous work fairly among themselves...rather than haphazardly? As soon as you seek fairness and justice, you are back to balanced job complexes

(and pareconish remuneration and decision making) because
without these features people have no way to know what is
fair and just, nor any way to act on the knowledge. So a good
society doesn't leave justice to chance. Instead, society develops, over time, a set of jobs incorporating needed tasks in a
balanced way.

So now your person in a parecon has only one big
choice—to participate by working at some available balanced
job they like, or not.

9. Seeking Dignified Work

I would like to believe that people have an instinct for freedom, that they really want to control their own affairs. They don't want to be pushed around, ordered, oppressed, etc., and they want a chance to do things that make sense, like constructive work in a way that they control, or maybe control together with others. I don't know any way to prove this. It's really a hope about what human beings are like, a hope that if social structures change sufficiently, those aspects of human nature will be realized.
-Noam Chomsky

We want to dignify work so we seek to equalize the empowerment effects of all jobs. But how?

Upgrading the Bottom

Capitalism leads to dole queues, the scramble for markets, and war. Collectivism leads to concentration camps, leader worship, and war. There is no way out of this unless a planned economy can somehow be combined with the freedom of the intellect, which can only happen if the concept of right and wrong is restored to politics.
-George Orwell

Much work is intentionally down precisely so that workers don't gain confidence and knowledge that would help them make demands about conditions or wages. And the same holds for workers being systematically isolated from one another and denied interaction and sociality. All this degra- dation enhances control from above.

An initial move toward dignified work is to improve the circumstances, conditions, and options of those in the most menial jobs. We could demand improved conditions, a less stressful pace of work, better ventilation or other relevant improvements, plus allowances for ongoing education to get better work. Each workplace and job has its own unique details, of course, but still, in a workplace with many rote and boring positions, workers might usefully seek the right to trade tasks for variety, to increase workplace interaction for sociality, and to freely use inactive moments for creative engagement and learning rather than simply enduring boredom.

Lowering the Top

He, who before was the money owner, now strides in front as capitalist; the possessor of labor-power follows as his laborer. The one with an air of importance, smirking, intent on business; the other hesitant, like one who is bringing his own hide to market and has nothing to expect but—a hiding.
-Karl Marx

Moving toward balanced job complexes includes not only bettering the lot of the worst off, but also allocating some onerous tasks to those with a monopoly of desirable and empowering responsibilities. Think of a law firm. There already exists the interesting concept of pro bono legal work. Firm members donate a certain amount of their energies to the indigent as a social responsibility. Campaigns to dignify work can also benefit from having those with elite jobs do tasks they otherwise would not have opted for. Thus, we might demand that those who have enjoyable and empowering work must reallocate some of their time to tasks ordinarily lower in the hierarchy in their workplaces, thereby allowing those with less fortunate work assignments the time to pursue better options.

Lawyers would spend some time doing tasks for their secretaries or for those who clean the building, freeing the latter to enjoy on the job training, etc. Or nurses, orderlies, and custodians could demand time for further training, less stress, better conditions, and more sociality, and the doctors and administrators in their hospitals could have to make up at least part of the labor difference. Just thinking about it, don't you find yourself smiling?

Creating A New Middle

I and the public know
What all schoolchildren learn
That those to whom evil is don,
Do evil in return.
-W. H. Auden

Seeking to have secretaries and custodians, nurses and orderlies, or workers doing rote labor on assembly lines or waiting tables in restaurants benefit from better conditions or get a little extra time for new training, and having those hierarchically above them in their workplaces do some onerous tasks to make up for losses, of course, would be very good. But an even better approach would literally change the tasks that people do. We could demand, for example, that owners give workers in lower positions more information processing tasks, more tasks that give confidence and develop decision-making skills, and more decision-making tasks per se, while reducing the amount of these same tasks in the jobs of those in higher administrative and policy-making positions.

Thus, nurses and custodians and assembly workers and cooks and waitresses and delivery drivers assess their workplaces and demand reallocation of tasks and responsibilities from the jobs of those hierarchically above them into their own job definitions, with some of their onerous tasks in turn

going upward. As a result, job requirements become more humane and empowering, and move toward being balanced.

Secretaries demand more diverse empowering responsibilities that give them more time in intellectual and deci-
sion-related functions. Waiters redefine waiting on tables to
be more interactive and social and less servile. They demand
new conditions and social relations, as well as more decision-making power in their restaurants.

All this probably sounds vague—but that's proper at this
stage of discussion. There are few if any general rules about
such matters. The issue is for those employed in each firm to
use their councils to reassess their work and raise demands to
reallocate components of work more fairly than when they are
allocated to dehumanize, atomize, and disempower most employees, and elevate only a few.

Emphasizing Power

> *In every cry of every man,*
> *In every infant's cry of fear,*
> *In every voice, in every ban,*
> *The mind-forged manacles I bear.*
> *- William Blake*

The central issue in balancing jobs is ensuring that by virtue
of their economic lives all employees are comparably prepared
to participate in decision-making and have comparable access
to decision-making involvement. Thus, the best and most critical alterations to seek on the road to dignified work are those
impacting empowerment. Workers must especially seek reforms that spread access to knowledge and information, that
enlarge day-to-day social interactions, that enhance decision-making skills, and that win increased direct decision-making influence.

Instead of only doctors being involved in discussions and
decisions about hospital policy, this "task" is re-allocated
among doctors, nurses, and orderlies. Instead of managers be-

ing a separate category alone in possession of relevant deci-sion-making information and opportunities in factories, redefinitions distribute responsibilities and information among all workers, thereby reducing hierarchies of power.

Dignifying Our Own Work

> *Let us learn this lesson well because the fate of*
> *revolution depends upon it. "You shall reap what*
> *you sow" is the acme of all human wisdom and experience.*
> *-Alexander Berkman*

For organizations and movements to effectively advocate bal-anced job complexes in society, they will have to address their own internal job complexes as well. For one thing, who is go-ing to seek just work assignments at GM and then passively do only rote tasks in his or her union or other movement orga-nization? And who outside such a movement will be impressed if it doesn't practice what it preaches? "You say you are for bal-anced job complexes. Then why don't you have them?"

Think about *The Nation, Mother Jones*, Greenpeace, The Institute for Policy Studies, NOW, the NAACP, labor unions, massive peace movements, local housing campaigns, the New Party, and whatever other progressive or left institutions or movements you wish to bring into focus. In each case you might ask whether they have balanced job complexes or whether they have typical corporate divisions of labor so that some folks monopolize fulfilling and empowering tasks while others have only rote and obedient ones. If, the latter situation pertains, do the folks doing onerous jobs get paid more? Will the movement "owners," "CEOs," and "managers" welcome demands from their workforces to balance movement circum-stances for empowerment effects? Will they reallocate tasks in a steady progression toward balanced job complexes, includ-ing reducing their own elite prerogatives? In some cases the answer will be yes, but not always. However, the central issue isn't assuaging the worries of those now administering movement organizations. It is attaining a movement that practices what it preaches economically, a movement that benefits its members, improves its product, becomes congenial to working class constituencies, and makes credible its external demands, all by attaining balanced job complexes in its own organizations.

Just as blacks and latinos and women in movement projects, organizations, and campaigns have had a responsibility to push, cajole, and struggle the movement forward on matters of internal race and gender relations over the past few decades, so too do those who now occupy the rote and lowly "working class" positions of our movement organizations have a responsibility to push, cajole, and struggle the movement forward on matters of internal class definition. The strategic focuses and demands noted throughout this chapter for society apply as well to our own institutions, though we can hope that the struggle inside our institutions will be quicker, completed soon, and able to provide a solid foundation for larger subsequent struggles outside our institutions.

10. Participatory Allocation

Buying and selling is essentially antisocial.
-Edward Bellamy

The only possible alternative to being either the oppressed
or the oppressor is voluntary cooperation for the good of all.
-William   Von Humboldt

A n economy needs some procedure for coordinating different workers' activities with one another and with the desires of consumers. The procedure, called economic allocation,
determines how much of each input and output is used or produced, and where it winds up.

The current overwhelming consensus is that markets are a
worthy economic allocation institution. Some dissidents still
support central planning instead. In our view, however, both
markets and central planning are abysmal and we need participatory planning as an alternative. Beyond what a short
chapter can argue, I hope folks will pursue the more substantial arguments available at http://www.parecon.org

Markets, No

Few markets can ever have been as competitive as those
that flourished in Britain in the first half of the
nineteenth century, when infants became deformed

*as they toiled their way to an early death in the pits
and mills of the Black Country. And there is no lack of
examples today to confirm the fact also that well-functioning
markets have no innate tendency to promote excellence
in any form. They offer no resistance to forces making
for a descent into cultural barbarity or moral depravity.*

-Robert Solo

Markets involve buyers and sellers coming together with
each trying to maximize his or her own benefit. In any transaction the buyer and seller compete to buy cheap and sell dear.
For one to get more, the other must get less. Those affected by
the transaction but not directly involved as buyer or seller
have no say in it. Pollution or other effects on non-buyer/sell-
ers go unaccounted for and can't influence the transaction.
Even with markets that are working optimally, actors become
individualist. Their motives and preference development are
skewed toward me-firstism. No wonder "nice guys finish last."
Exchange rates ignore social and external effects and therefore diverge from true social costs. A class division emerges
between those few "coordinators" who monopolize decision-making skills, opportunities, and information, and a
much larger group of workers disenfranchised from decision
making. The coordinators, with owners, rule the economy.
The workers follow orders.

In these ways and others, markets cause people to trample
one another's well being. They homogenize tastes within
classes and reduce all activity to the cash nexus. They remunerate power or output, creating grotesque income differentials, and allot disproportionate power to a class that
monopolizes decision-making access at the expense of the majority who only follow orders.

Central Planning, No

*Just as the functions of the bodily organs of plants
and animals cannot be arbitrarily altered, so that, for*

example, one cannot at will hear with his eyes and see with his ears, so one also cannot at pleasure transform an organ of social repression into an instrument for the liberation.
-Rudolf Rocker

Central planning is conceptually simpler than market allocation. Planners accumulate information by diverse means and then decide exchange rates, amounts to produce, and incomes. Workers and consumers abide the planners' decisions. The only wrinkle is that the planners have to issue orders and get some feedback on their possibility...orders go down, feedback comes back up, orders go down, obedience comes back up. The feedback comes from "agents" of the planners in each workplace, the managers and other members of the coordinator class.

On the plus side, central planning can conceivably overcome the intrinsic inability of markets to account for the social and public implications of transactions and can also conceivably reduce the individualizing effects of market competition and even take into account production and consumption effects on workers and consumers. But an inherent problem is that central planning inevitably produces coordinator class rule with planners allying with their managerial agents in each workplace to in turn control rote workers while also adding generalized authoritarianism and subordination to economics, thereby strongly violating self-management. The class dynamics and increased authoritarianism of central planning tend over time to swamp the technical potential it has to pay better attention to generalized social and personal development. Instead in practice central planning biases outcomes toward the enhancement of the power, status, and conditions of elite planners, managers, and other educated coordinator class members, at the expense of workers.

Markets and central planning therefore not only don't promote just rewards, self-management, and dignified work, they severely impede their achievement, even as they also undermine solidarity, diversity, and other civilized social norms.

Participatory Planning, Yes

> *In the individual expression of my own life I would*
> *have brought about the immediate expression of your life,*
> *and so in my individual activity I would have directly*
> *confirmed and realized my authentic nature, my human,*
> *communal nature. Our productions would be as many*
> *mirrors from which our natures would shine forth.*
> *This relation would be mutual: what applies to me*
> *would also apply to you. My labor would be*
> *the free expression and hence the enjoyment of life.*
> *-Karl Marx*

So what's our alternative? Well, why can't workers in different enterprises and industries, and consumers in different neighborhoods and regions, coordinate their joint endeavors themselves—consciously, democratically, equitably, and efficiently? Why can't councils of consumers and workers propose what they would like to do, and revise their own proposals as they discover more about the impact of their desires on others? What is impossible about a social, multi-step planning procedure in which other workers approve production proposals only when, in light of full qualitative information and accurate valuations, they are convinced the proposals are socially efficient, and in which other consumers approve consumption requests only when, in light of full information, they are convinced the requests are not socially abusive? What is impossible, in other words, about the associated producers and consumers together planning their related activities without the debilitating effects of markets or central planning?

We have already argued for workers' and consumers' councils and federations of councils, for remuneration according to effort and sacrifice, for balanced job complexes, and for actors to influence decisions in proportion as they are affected by them.

The participants in participatory planning will be individual workers and consumers, the workers' and consumers' councils and federations, and various groups of people a part of whose balanced job complex is to do data handling to assist allocation. They will work in what we call "Iteration Facilitation Boards" (IFBs).

Conceptually, the participatory planning procedure is pretty simple, but quite different than anything we are accustomed to. Workers and consumers negotiate outcomes based on full knowledge of effects. They have proportionate influence in decisions. The facilitation board announces what we call "indicative prices" for all goods, resources, categories of labor, and capital stocks. These indicative prices are calculated based on the prior year's experience and knowledge of general changes since. Consumers, consumer councils, and federations respond with consumption proposals, taking the indicative prices as estimates of a true valuation of all the resources, equipment, labor, bad byproducts, and social benefits associated with each good or service. Workers, workers councils, and council federations simultaneously offer production proposals, listing the outputs they would make available and the inputs they would need to produce them, taking the indicative prices as estimates of the full social benefits of outputs and costs of all inputs. Receiving the public proposals from workers, consumers, and their councils, the facilitation boards calculate the excess demand or supply for each good and mechanically adjust the indicative price for the good up or down in light of the new data and in accord with socially agreed formulas for these alterations. Then, using the new indicative prices, taking account of the first round of production and consumption proposals, plus full qualitative information, consumer and worker councils and federations revise and resubmit their proposals, in a second round.

Essentially the back and forth procedure "whittles" overly optimistic, infeasible proposals down to a feasible plan in which what is offered by producers matches what is sought by consumers in two different ways: Consumers requesting more than their effort ratings (income) warrant, or together wanting more of some good than workers propose to produce, are pressured by new indicative prices and the desire to attain a viable final plan to reduce or shift requests to less socially costly items. These requests garner the approval of other consumer councils, who regard their prior requests as excessive, or of workers reluctant to supply the outputs previously sought. Workers' councils whose proposals have lower than average social benefit given the resources at their disposal or who are proposing less than consumers desire of their product, are pressured to increase either their efforts or their efficiency (or their number of employees) to win the approval of other workers and meet consumer desires. In other words, if you are asking for too much stuff relative to your income, or if groups want too much of some item collectively, or if as a worker your workplace isn't producing sufficiently for its available assets or there is more desire for what you are producing than you have accounted for, you raise or lower your proposals in accord. The goals is to get your proposals to an acceptable range, on the one hand, and to facilitate arriving at a viable plan, on the other. As a consumer, your income is a function of your effort and sacrifice at work. As a producer or workplace, the output expected from your firm is a function of the productive capacity of the assets you are employing.

As each round of the planning process proceeds, or with each iteration, in the technical parlance, proposals move closer to mutual feasibility while (and because) indicative prices converge toward true social opportunity costs, which is to say, true representations of the actual benefits and costs associated with the production and consumption of each economic item. Since no participant in the planning procedure enjoys an advantage in influence over any other, and since each participant impacts the valuation of social costs and benefits like all others do, but with each having more impact on what they are involved in producing and consuming and less on what they aren't affected by, the procedure generates equity, efficiency, and self-management simultaneously.

In other words, individuals make proposals for their own private consumption. Neighborhood councils make proposals that include approved requests for private goods as well as shared requests for the neighborhood's collective consumption. Higher-level federations of consumer councils make proposals that include approved requests from member councils as well as the federation's collective consumption request.

Similarly, each production unit proposes a production plan. Workplaces enumerate the inputs they want and outputs they propose to make available. Regional and industry federations aggregate proposals and keep track of excess supply and demand. Having proposed its own plan, every "actor" (individual or collective) receives information regarding other actors' proposals and the response of other actors to its proposal. Each actor (individual or collective), then makes a new proposal. As every actor "bargains" through successive "iterations," reacting to "indicative prices," their own agreed measures of effort and sacrifice, and detailed qualitative information from one another available on request, the process converges to a viable plan.

The attained plan manifests actors' preferences proportionately as they are impacted. More, each actor benefits only insofar as do all others. That is, my income depends directly on the socially average income (I get somewhat more or somewhat less due to my contributing a greater or lesser amount of effort and sacrifice than average) and my job comfort depends on the quality of the socially average job complex (since we all have a balanced job complex, each equal to the others in quality of life and empowerment impact). Even my benefit from any investment I propose for my own workplace depends on how that investment raises social averages for jobs or alters average income by expanding the total social product that we all share in—and so does yours.

Solidarity is therefore enhanced by participatory planning because our interests are entwined and our daily economic calculations occur in light of one another's situations. For my income to go up, either I have to expend more effort and sacrifice, or the social average has to go up with everyone benefitting. For the quality of my work situation to improve, the quality of society's balanced job complex must improve, and thus everyone's situation must improve. Diversity is fostered to gain the benefits that accrue from many options and checks and balances. Equity is guaranteed by the remunerative norm. Self-management is intrinsic to the allocation system's foundational logic and operation, fostered by its every feature.

To clarify the process, prices are "indicative" during the planning process in the sense of indicating the best current estimates of final valuations. These indicative prices are not binding at each stage, but are instead flexible guides in that everyone knows that they may change in a future round of planning, but also in that qualitative information provides important additional guidance that can lead people to act contrary to what quantitative prices indicate. More, the indicative prices up to and including the final rates of exchange do not stem from competition between buyers and sellers trying to fleece one another or from authoritarian determinations biased toward the well-being of the decision makers, but from social consultation and compromise. The appended qualitative information comes directly from concerned parties and enters the process to help keep the quantitative indicators as accurate as possible, as well as to develop workers' and consumers' sensitivity to fellow workers' and consumers' situations and everyone's understanding of the intricate tapestry of human relations that determines what we can and cannot consume or produce.

Obviously, the above just touches the surface of participatory planning...not providing a detailed picture of either the planning "iterations" or the background of motives, actions, and institutions that make them viable, nor elaborating on the day-to-day roles nor social implications. But if interested you can certainly access more comprehensive discussions at http://www.parecon.org. The main point is that the balancing of what is produced and what is consumed in light of the relative costs and benefits that go into each part of the equation, can be achieved cooperatively rather than via methods that distort both personalities and outcomes. It can be attained in accord with self-management and fostering diversity, solidarity, and equity, rather than violating all these values.

In the next chapter we will address short-term program for attaining participatory planning. For now, however, regarding a vision for allocation...it comes down to this.

- Do we want to let people have income in accord with capital ownership or power or try to measure the value of each person's contribution to social production and allow individuals to withdraw consumption goods in accord with their output? Or do we want to base any differences in consumption rights only on differences in personal sacrifices made in producing goods and services? In other words, do we want an economy that implements the maxim "to each according to the value of his or her property or power or personal contribution," or an economy that obeys the maxim "to each according to his or her effort?"

- Do we want a few to conceive and coordinate the work of the many? Or do we want everyone to have the opportunity to participate in economic decision making to the degree they are affected by the outcome, and the training and circumstances to guarantee their capacity to do so? In other words, do we want to continue to organize work hierarchically, or do we want job complexes balanced for empowerment?

- Do we want a structure for expressing preferences biased in favor of individual over social consumption? Or do we want to make it as easy to register preferences for social as for individual consumption? In other words, do we want atomistic consumers or nested federations of consumer councils?

- And do we want economic decisions to be determined by groups competing against one another for well-being and survival, the enhancement of any one being attained only at the expense of some other? Or do we want to plan our joint endeavors democratically, equitably, and efficiently, with all actors having the proper influence and each benefiting in parallel with the rest? In other words, do we want to abdicate economic decision making to the market, or do we want to embrace the possibility of participatory planning?

11. Q&A: Participatory Allocation

*As it happens, there are no columns in standard
double-entry book-keeping to keep track of satisfaction
and demoralization. There is no credit entry for feelings
of self-worth and confidence, no debit column for
feelings of uselessness and worthlessness. There are no
monthly, quarterly, or even annual statements of pride
and no closing statement of bankruptcy when the
worker finally comes to feel that after all he couldn't
do anything else, and doesn't deserve anything better.*
-Barbara Garson

Is It A Market?

- *Is a parecon really a non-market economy? It seems to me
  that the heart of it, the iterative negotiation process, is actually a market process.*

This question has been raised as well by a couple of economists, three or four years ago, if I remember right, in *Socialist Review* magazine. It only got raised once, because most
economists are so horrified by what we propose that they
would never see it this way, or because they perceive just how
different it is—I don't know which. Those two economists look
at participatory planning and see

a) There are numeric indicators we call indicative prices,
but which look quite like any price you have ever

known, which people and institutions consult to make their decisions.

b) The mix and match of the decisions people make come into accord, by a meshing of supply and demand.

You then deduce, as they do, that this is, after all, some kind of market system, prices and supply and demand being "market" features.

Well, the answer I offer depends on what we mean by "a market system."

If we mean a system in which there are any prices at all and in which supply and demand come into accord, then, yes, you would be right. But by this logic, all non-trivial allocation systems would be "some kind of market system" (including even central planning which also has prices and supply and demand coming into accord) and instead of markets being a specific kind of allocation mechanism, the word market would be a synonym for allocation itself, and we would need a new word for what economists more typically mean by a market system...

More, when you use the term "markets" in that very encompassing way, which many people do, it makes folks think that having markets is essentially inevitable, so that what we have in the U.S. is essentially inevitable.

Suppose you looked at the Soviet Union some time back. You would see the same thing as what has caused you to identify parecon as some type of market system. Everything had a price. Supply and demand came into proximity, and it happened via a process that in large part took note of responses of actors to prices. Yet you wouldn't have called it a market economy, I think, quite rightly.

Any economy beyond direct personal barter includes some kind of mechanism for people to make comparisons among options (including some kind of prices perhaps accompanied, as in our parecon case, by qualitative information as well) and if it isn't horribly wasteful, any such system also involves supply and demand coming into proximity of one another, as did the

Soviet economy. But no one would mistake the old Soviet economy for a market economy, nonetheless.

Why? Well, because the Soviet institutional framework and its components, and in particular the roles for each actor in allocation established by these institutions, were quite different than those that define what we call market exchange. In the Soviet Union, prices were ultimately set by planners (who did, however, consult people's reactions to those prices). The workers had only to respond regarding their ability to fulfill instructions and to convey information about available resources, etc., as well as to obey instructions. The planners had only to calculate and set prices and issue marching orders. Managers had to administer as well as obey. Consumers had to go to the store and pick what they wanted to consume, paying the established price and keeping within their budget—seemingly quite like at A&P in the U.S. And so on.

My point is that, yes, parecon has, among other features, a kind of prices, a kind of budgeting, and a meshing of supply and demand. But, nonetheless, it is not a market system because it not only doesn't have the basic defining features of markets—buyers and sellers each motivated to maximize their own advantage at the cost of the other; competitively determined prices; profit or surplus maximization; remuneration to labor according to its bargaining power or its output—but because it has other features that are entirely contrary to these, such as balanced job complexes, worker and consumer councils, remuneration according to effort and sacrifice, participatory planning guided by human well being and development.

- *How would participatory planning take place accurately and without inefficiency?*

It would be an iterative (round by round) process in which what consumers want to receive matches up to what producers are ready to offer and each side steadily expands or diminishes its preferences until there is a mesh. The interchange would be facilitated by comprehensive quantitative and qualitative information concerning social costs and benefits of all production and consumption, both in text form (qualitative) and in what are called indicative prices (for calculation purposes). There are also various facilitating institutions that encapsulate and relay information. As to its efficiency properties (would it waste anything people value) no economist has challenged these, perhaps because of the proofs we offer in our more technical presentations of the model.

Individual Participation and Local Effects

- *Would individuals really have to itemize their expenditures months in advance? Why the necessity for individuals to take part in detailed planning?*

Individuals would partake as well as other size units, but for a year, and, as you imagine, it would be largely based on past years, and on projections for changes in overall output and in each individual's share for the year, etc.

Any system that has any connection to actual humans must, of course, respond to human choices. Markets do this daily. Parecon gets a prior indication of totals, a good one, during the yearly planning period. There are many reasons for this. Suppose you are in a local community that could as a collective, buy a new park, or new joint music equipment, or large computers for a kids center, or whatever. Such collective consumption is charged against the incomes of all the community members ,of course. So getting more means getting less individual consumption, and getting less of the collectively enjoyed items means getting more individual consumption. So, one reason for planning with a longer period at stake is to decide on this ratio. Another thing to be aware of is possible changes in output, and thus income. Another is changes in taste, particularly for new outputs. And so on. But all this adjustment is manageable in participatory planning, and consistently with our values (as is described in considerable detail in longer works on the vision, such as *Looking Forward* (SEP).

- *How transparent would the whole consumption and facilitation process be? Is individual privacy maintained?*

All the component calculations and sorting done by such boards would be on record and easy to check—not simply the final data sorted and summarized information that is plugged back into the planning process. This isn't very important, I think, as a guard against ill-doing, not only because parecon would have gentle people, but because in a parecon it would be virtually impossible even for someone intent on doing so and with no qualms about it, to misuse their role at a facilitation board. What the availability of facilitation boards' data and ruminations would be useful for, however, is learning about past algorithms to make improvements in the future.

Personal consumption requests, however, would presumably be private, though the requests could be be accessed without the accompanying names. (This choice of privacy, like many other choices one might make about a parecon, isn't somehow intrinsic to being a parecon, though—at least in my thinking. That is, I think one could have a parecon with all requests publicly accessible or not, with no effect on the defining economy per se, though other issues people may care a lot about are at stake. I think privacy is preferable but it isn't intrinsic to parecon, only quite consistent with it.)

- *Would parecon allow small-time marketing? Someone going off and doing their thing?*

Would there be smaller production units and larger ones? Sure. But there would be no marketing in the sense that it exists now. There would be no sales aimed at volume/profits rather than at fulfillment/use. No one would have any interest in having someone consume something unless the consumer benefits thereby.

- *There are a lot of things that could never be bargained or planned for on a yearly basis. Wouldn't some kind of market system work better to distribute those items?*

Why do you think there are such things? If you mean one can't know in advance that one will want a product that only arrives as an option six months later—say a book not yet published, for example—sure. But you can know that last year you got x books and your prediction, flexible and updateable as the year proceeds, is that this year you will want y more or less than last year (perhaps due to having more or less time for reading, or a change in your taste, etc.) And similarly for other choices; sometimes your expectations are quite precise, sometimes they are general and broad. Individuals don't know the precise clothes they will want (new designs, etc.) but can say, pretty closely (with up and down fluctuations across many people averaging to near zero change for the total request), what overall clothes expenditures they anticipate making. (All this kind of thing is dealt with in considerable detail in the longer books on the model such as SEP's *Looking Forward* or PUP's *Political Economy of Participatory Economics*, by the way.)

Of course one doesn't plan for the whimsical personal purchase, or items that are just not known about in advance (responses to illness, for example). But one can in broad terms indicate the parts of one's income that will go to this and that area—sometimes only broadly, sometimes in detail (e.g. wanting a new vehicle or other large items). When averaged over communities and societies, this data becomes powerful information that translates into requests for products that exist alongside offers of production from the workplaces, which then must be brought into alignment by a back and forth modifying of desires in light of continually updated information.

Allocation Details - Creeping Authority?

- *How would the "facilitation institutions" work?*

Each actor (which is sometimes an individual, sometimes a unit—such as a workplace or a community council, etc.) would enter a proposal for their economic activity, that is, for what they wish to take in (consume or in any event receive) and for what they wish to give out (that is, to produce).

These proposals obviously wouldn't mesh into a workable plan right off. In all likelihood, for most goods there would be more desired than offered—even when people were trying to make sensible proposals based on projections of the likely average income for the coming period and on awareness of their past period's actual results. The demands would be brought into touch with the supplies and vice versa by a decentralized process of refining proposals in light of data from prior rounds of proposals, technical data about capabilities, etc.

Facilitation Boards would be workplaces like any others in the economy. They would have various tasks, combined into job complexes. If the Facilitation Board's average job complex were better than the average for society, people working there part of their time would have to work at sub-average options outside. If it were worse than for the rest of society, then people working there would have to work at better than average tasks outside the board itself, some time each week

- *What does a board do?*

Basically they accumulate proposals and information more generally, work on the data to prepare it for access by others sometimes using various algorithms socially agreed upon to cull insights from it. This might be to help the planning process itself, to help people find available jobs, etc. That is it. No decisions. Also, everything they do can be checked and evaluated by anyone. All the information received and processed is accessible. Moreover, as far as we can tell, virtually everything they do could be largely and perhaps completely automated, at least in theory.

- *Surely you are starting to imply a coordinator class, if a small one, just by having people working in an institution whose role would be to decide who is affected by a certain decision and to what degree?*

No. The planning process has no need for anyone to play such a role as you indicate—the proportionate impacts emerge organically, not by being decreed by someone or some group.

However, just to take up the underlying concern you raise, suppose such estimates did have to be made. That does not inexorably mean there would be a coordinator class in an economy any more than does there being a managerial function in some industries, or an engineering function, or a surgical one, or a need to have agencies that do important calculations or summarize important information, mean that folks involved in those activities will be a separate and privileged class. If everyone has a balanced job complex, then no one has disproportionately more empowering work than others...so no one does only this type work...even though the specialized and empowering and consequential work does get done. Moreover, if there are no ways to make aggrandizing decisions for oneself or for a separate class by virtue of doing such work as a part of one's job complex, then abuse of even temporary powers is virtually impossible, certainly in any systematic way that leads to on-going structural hierarchies of wealth or power. This is all dealt with in great detail, down to workplace circumstances, in *Looking Forward* (SEP), with examples, etc., but I hope the idea is clear enough.

- *But if I work in an institution which controls some of the critical levers of the economy, even if I have a balanced job complex within that institution, I may still not have a balanced job complex with regard to economic power and the broader community, right?*

Well, what is this institution that you have in mind to work in and thereby benefit from? And what advantages does it bestow upon you, and others like you working in it, such that you are a class with advantages to defend and enlarge? Your fear is valid enough in the abstract, of course, since it could be the case, in some economy. But having agreed on that, then we need to see whether in any particular economy this thing you are concerned about exists in practice.

For example, if you were a central planner, in a centrally planned economy, able to bend and influence economic outcomes to serve your class, the coordinator class, which has its own separate and elite position in the economy, by further enlarging the advantages it enjoys due to promoting investment patterns that enhance information centralization and thus the further aggrandizement of intellectual workers or coordinator class members—your claim would be quite right. But, this doesn't exist in parecon.

Yes, there would be bureaus in parecon that disseminate and even summarize information, but there would be no way for anyone working in one of these institutions to benefit themselves or some group by doing anything other than what is also in everyone else's interest, that is, doing the work as well as they can. For one thing any deviation would be obvious. But, even more important, aside from trivia, no deviation could be self-serving. It is precisely this kind of attribute that is rather striking about parecon, in fact.

It is ultimately quite simple—to improve one's economic lot one needs more income or better circumstances (more power does it too, by allowing the other two aims to be met). But, in parecon, everyone would get a share of income based on the effort and sacrifice they expend in work (and on need if they can't work) which means there would be no way to aggrandize oneself or a group without, in fact, benefitting everyone. For me to get ahead, the total product must grow or I have to expend more effort and sacrifice, which is fair enough. I can't get ahead at the expense of others.

Similarly, since we all would have balanced job complexes, my work situation would only improve if the society's average job complex improved, if everyone's situation at work benefitted. Groups don't compete for economic power or income.

I suppose you could make some kind of case for a sector of fakers who make believe they can't work and consume the average bundle anyhow....but it is quite far fetched. And they would not be ruling anyone, and since to get away with it, they would have to show all the signs of a work-preventing ailment, they would likely suffer as much as they would gain.

- *How would a new venture get started under Parecon? Would an (or a group of) entrepreneur(s) make a proposal to a production council or group of councils and hope to be granted the resources to start up their company?*

A group of "enterprising" workers—not entrepreneurs as the word is literally defined—would apply to the federation of workers' councils in their industry for the federations' "approval" to be a workers' council and submit proposals in the participatory planning process, which in turn is how one asks for, and perhaps receives, resources and inputs. The federations would okay the group as having requisite competence and experience—essentially as a "serious" group that should be allowed to make work proposals. In capitalism, banks asked to lend money to an entrepreneur ask for business plans, credentials, etc. In a parecon it would be the industry federation that would do something similar. And the industry federation would also sometimes try to stimulate or organize groups of workers to start up new enterprises—always run as parecon workers' councils. The difference between the banks and the industry federations is the former are looking for profit possibilities, and the latter are looking for social desirability.

- *If the enterprise fails, would the entire group suffer the consequences or only the original participants?*

A workers' council "fails" if it cannot get a work proposal approved during the participatory planning process—or if it fails to deliver promised outputs and those who were supposed to get deliveries convince the industry federation that this is a chronic and irredeemable problem. This would usually only happen after the industry federation had already arranged for some key workers from a successful workers' council to visit and work temporarily at the failing enterprise, and/or workers at the failing enterprise had been sent to work at successful ones—in an attempt to get the failing enterprise "up to snuff." Since the best techniques are available and free for all to use, there is no reason one council could not duplicate the

efforts of others. But....if the enterprise does fail, then the
workers look for jobs elsewhere—aided by a robust and humane version of training, retraining, and job search, with average income in place. In other words, suffering is minimal.

- *I understand in terms of consumption that each person is
  remunerated in proportion to sacrifice—that is, hours
  worked and unpleasantness of work compared to average. For the most part there is very little variance from
  average. Effort and sacrifice, yes. We work at balanced
  job complexes. Therefore, if you work at one for 4 hours,
  and I work at one for 4 hours, and we both work at an acceptable non-shirking pace, we are each going to get the
  same pay despite our job complexes having different components. But as I understand it, the workplace pays
  someone (the labor facilitation board?) for the actual
  marginal value of the labor, that is, according to output.*

Not quite. In calculations product value is taken into account
so that the workplace has to utilize its assets well. But people
are not paid for their output.

The details of the planning process can get a little technical. If you want to delve into it, I suggest the Princeton book,
Political Economy of Participatory Economics. The broad
point, sufficient for understanding and assessment, however,
is that labor receives pay for effort and sacrifice in balanced
job complexes. At the same time, you don't want workplaces
having highly productive workforces or other assets putting in
proposals to generate output that would take less effort (due
to their greater productive human or other resources) than
other workplaces are proposing to expend, thus leaving the
workers to loaf or otherwise underutilizing assets. Thus, the
planning process has to "charge" workplaces for the productive capabilities of all assets, including workers. This is one of
the only difficult aspects of the parecon model and logic. Technically the details are quite important to outcomes, but politically and socially they are uninstructive.

- *Given the complexity of the medical industry and the provision of medical services, allocation of health care on a societal level seems to be much more involved than other industries. Could you sketch how health care would be allocated in a parecon system?*

People, except for unusual instances, can't say "this year I want such and such health care." It is not something planned on the basis of preferences espoused by individuals in the way that bicycles or peanuts are. Rather, the "demand side" is essentially a calculation for society. We know, from past history and trends, roughly how much health a given level of spending will achieve, how much prevention and treatment in a coming year. So depending on our estimates of sickness and what we want to achieve in preventing and treating it, weighed against the cost in resources and effort, we settle on a societal health care plan. While health care goes to individuals, it is, nonetheless, a social and completely public good re the demand side. It is paid for by everyone via a reduction of total available goods equal to what is allotted to health care. Health care goes to those who need it, however.

So I don't think health raises any insurmountable problems for parecon. Health producers propose supply, citizens organized at the societal level request what they want—these come into balance, as with other products and industries. Providers work in balanced job complexes, like everyone.

Black Markets and Re-emerging Capitalism

- *Why couldn't someone decide to operate outside the planning process and thereby subvert its operations for their personal gain?*

Could one person trade items to another outside the participatory planning process? Sure, in principle. But when benign, that is just bartering, not production and sale, and presumably it would be equitable and inconsequential.

But to follow your concerns further, suppose we have the equivalent of Mozart in our community. Can she sit in her abode and write music and then go outside and auction it off to the highest bidder?

No. And the same holds if we had a Picasso. He can't make paintings and then sell them off privately, becoming fantastically wealthy. This is not permitted.

These individuals get the benefit of society's roads, infrastructure, and so on and so forth. They abide its role offerings like all other folks. They work and get income like others, for effort and sacrifice, not the value of their output.

Remuneration is not according to the social value of one's product/contribution (in which case this contemporary Picasso or Mozart would grow rich), but according to the effort and sacrifice expended in producing valued product. And folks must also work at balanced job complexes (so even the contemporary art or other genius has to do their fair share of different tasks in their job complex), because balanced jobs are the only ones that exist within the economy.

- *But isn't parecon vulnerable to re-emerging capitalism? Let's say that a country is adapted to parecon. An individual, one very skilled tailor, finds that people appreciate his work, and that he can charge them for favors. Soon, the tailor has made such a profit that he can give pay to other tailors to do his work on a larger scale, and after a while he has established an industry. With his profits, his empire can freely expand. Capitalism is reinstated.*

This is a black market and one can imagine lots of different approaches to the issue in different parecons. At the extremes one society might decide, this is such a minuscule problem we will simply ignore it institutionally, letting normal operations reduce it to a trivial annoyance, but taking no special steps. Another society might make non-planning transfers illegal beyond some low amount (effectively allowing barter of goods among actors, but not business).

For you to think about which you would favor of these po-
lar positions or anything in between...you might want to take
into account a few things.

(1) The second part of the problem, hiring wage slaves with
lucre gained from black marketeering, is simply not an option
in parecon. At an absolute minimum, the economy will not allot resources to a production unit assembled in such a fashion—not to mention, why would anyone work there?

Make the problem more real. A country goes parecon, another hasn't. A rich person from the latter comes into the
parecon and advertises for wage slaves to work in a factory of
his, that he wants to build in the parecon country, at a high
pay rate, let's say. Why can't this happen? On the one hand, if
you believe in parecon you think most folks will look at this
guy like the devil and want nothing to do with him. On the
other hand, what if some folks, for whatever reasons, want to
give up balanced job complexes and remuneration according
to effort and sacrifice and having impact on decisions and
council democracy, and so on, for better wages (and you might
think through whether this guy can possibly make big profits
paying wages sufficient to attract people away from parecon
firms)? Well, society just doesn't allow it. It won't provide the
firm with inputs, it won't accept its outputs, again, at a minimum.

(2) But what about the first part of the problem you
raise—for example I have these wonderful trinkets that I
make in my spare time from (it can't be inputs that I'd have to
get from the economy) road kill or stuff I go dig up or find in
the trash, or whatever...or, to make it more real...I am a mind
bogglingly good tennis player or pianist and I sell lessons or
games on the sly. It is technically possible, but very hard in
practice. You can't transfer income—actual money—because
(a) it isn't an option and (b) the black marketeer couldn't enter
the planning process to consume with it without revealing, by
its magnitude, that he/she was cheating. So the black marketeer has to be paid in kind—in goods, that is just as if he
traded his sweater for his neighbors shoes, but in this case
trading a service, like tennis lessons. It's very clumsy, to say

the least, thus putting an upper lid on the problem even without taking into account the social onus. But in fact, how does the black marketeer explain his/her abundance (if he/she manages to get people to provide it)? The social ostracism that would accompany any cheating revealed by ostentatious consumption would be a very high price to pay for marginal income above and beyond an already quite comfortable and socially rich existence. And this price isn't only social and moral in a parecon. Much consumption is collective, and that would be lost as well.

The point is, even without legal penalties, on the one side there is great difficulty carrying off the behavior you indicate and accruing much by way of it. On the other side, there is considerable loss in being identified as a social ingrate (which is almost impossible to avoid if you are benefitting significantly).

Now, going back to the original social choice, believing all the above, assuming it makes sense to you, you might figure it isn't worth society's time to bother worrying about this problem. It is easier to just turn the other cheek and if some folks manage a little lucre, so be it. Or you might decide that the dangers are real and substantial and that society ought to police the matter. Or, perhaps, you might move from the latter view to the former view as the system develops, as parecon consciousness and values become commonplace, etc.

- *Should we stop black markets, and if so, how would we enforce and legislate against black markets?*

Is it right or wrong for a person to not have the option to garner the highest possible income that he/she can garner by trade of his/her talents? Of course if you think folks should be remunerated according to what they can extract (that is, according to bargaining power, which is what markets do) or according to their contribution to output (which is what markets are supposed to do) then you don't want parecon in the first place, because it remunerates according to effort and sacrifice. If you do want a parecon, then you wouldn't think it wrong to preclude black market profiteering.

As to restrictions per se—there is no such thing as "anything goes" in any society. It can't be "anything goes" for you and for me the minute I want to do x which precludes your doing y or vice versa. If you have institutions in a society, and there is no society that doesn't have institutions, then by virtue of the roles they embody and those they don't embody, even without laws, there are restrictions.

We don't allow slave-owning in the U.S. It is not permitted. It doesn't matter if I come to you with a million dollars and say sign here, be my slave—it isn't legal. But in fact, it isn't really an issue. The law is moot. No one wants to be a slave, no one wants slaves—the social opprobrium on both sides is too great, relative to the gains, even for venal, vile folks to attempt it. Now, having wage slaves is another matter—that is acceptable and therefore pursued with vigor and in fact is just taken as a natural given.

In parecon, by contrast, having wage slaves isn't an option. There are no roles in the society for it. You can't be part of the economy as a wage slave or be the employer of a wage slave. Such an actor would not get inputs and your outputs wouldn't be distributed. And if you try and do it on the sly, it is like trying to own a slave in a democratic, post-slavery, moderately enlightened capitalism on the sly. It is unacceptable and unlikely to succeed to any degree.

Parecon does not eliminate by definition or by consciousness-raising every violation of its own morals that someone might entertain. And your question is an apt form of a broader one—does parecon make violations of the values of parecon so counterproductive as to be not worth pursuing, for the most part, even if you could get away with it, and can it prosecute other violations, when they occur, as successfully as any other model prosecutes violations?

I think the answer is yes, on both counts—actually better.

By the by, if your next question is, well, what about murder, theft, etc.—or what about the black market if you decide to prosecute actors—do these require police, and if so won't that lead right back to old fashioned coercion and hierarchy?

This is a question about polity, not economics, but my intuition is that, no, incorporating a police function is not tantamount to incorporating old fashioned coercion and hierarchy. Others may disagree, but like having allocation via participatory planning is superior to having allocation via markets and not the same old exploitation and alienation, I suspect accomplishing a police function via humane procedures will be different from what we endure now, but that we will need some such function, nonetheless.

Artists and Parecon

- *Wouldn't parecon limit individual artistic creativity by deciding what art to produce by referendum or committee?*

Do you think this because artists, like producers of vehicles, get resources to work with (outputs of other people's efforts) or are allotted income for their work (and a claim on the social product) only insofar as their work, overall, is respected in the economy? I don't see why it leads to your concern.

By (1) elevating diversity and self-management parecon greatly promotes attitudes conducive to each, and (2) by allocating resources and tools and time self-consciously, it removes the impact of power or maldistribution of voting rights on the allocations, reducing the built-in tendency for "popularity" to outweigh "innovation" without any real assessment being made of the value of innovation.

If you mean to point out that it would be within the purview of society to decree that some type of innovation is unwanted or unlikely to be successful and that resources shouldn't be given over to it—yes, that is true—for art as for innovation in, say, how to electrocute people better, or for that matter, how to make better ladders, or whatever. But the assumption that in a parecon the population would not want musical and artistic innovation pursued by those with talents and creativity in their own manner as they evolve their dispositions and talents, seems to me very dubious. I should think the opposite would be true, overwhelmingly.

What people currently like would be part of the issue in parecon—for sure. But it isn't the whole of it, of course. For one thing, smaller groups can like things a lot, making such endeavors worthwhile even though not widely appreciated. But also, at a moment in time, much of what is pursued—not only in art, but in many dimensions of life, say science, engineering, medical experimentation, etc.—is not yet appreciated beyond those who are trying to explore it (maybe not even entirely by them). Art is not special in this respect, in fact. So there is need for exploration and elaboration of art, music, and ideas and information and innovation more generally, all of which moves out beyond where taste currently is. Sure.

But there is nothing about parecon that precludes or even impedes this type exploration relative to any other model I am aware of, much less capitalism...quite the contrary.

Imagine a workplace for musicians. Society respects this workplace and includes it as part of the economy because it values music, including innovation. To work at this institution one has to be hired which likely entails demonstrating certain knowledge, talent, etc. The institution's budget is allocated internally to various activities, by its members, and therefore certainly not only to what a mass audience outside already likes. It really isn't much different in that respect than a workplace investigating new products or ideas, if you think about it.

- *But aren't artists with such public controls not really artists anymore?*

This notion that an artist is some special unique creature, with special rights, entirely eludes me. This is a claim made by all intellectual workers—folks in or wanting to be in what I call the coordinator class—regarding their own particular pursuits—art, math, management, whatever. Each sees their activity as warranting total autonomy from society or themselves, but never sees the claim as equally valid for others. Yet the claim is true for all and for none, in fact, depending on what it means.

There is a difference, that is, between being controlled publicly, which what the question worries about, and being part of a society and operating by its norms and thus having a say over outcomes in proportion as they affect one, but not more. A big difference.

- *The whole idea of being an artist seems contrary to the notion of producing "popular" art for mass appeal. What happens to an artist who makes unappealing art in parecon?*

Suppose I happen to like some kind of weird arrangement of items in my living room, and I like the setup changed daily, and it takes me an hour each day to do it, and it is hard work. Should I be able to earn my living in part doing that? It has no value for anyone else in society whatsoever...let's say.

I think not. I think I shouldn't be forbidden from doing it, of course. But it is my private pursuit and it is more consumption than it is production, and so it isn't worthy of being called part of a job complex. Now this isn't by definition in a parecon—which could decide otherwise for reasons I don't yet or maybe would never personally agree with. That is, a parecon's participants could actually allow and incorporate this type activity as work consistently with the norms of being a parecon, though I doubt one ever would.

Something similar happens for art, music, and also engineering, science, etc. Insofar as society is going to allocate pay (a claim on income) to any activity, it is going to want that activity to "count" as work, which means that overall, on average, it has socially beneficial outcomes. (There may be lots of misses on the road to some hits, or benefit may have many meanings...but still...)

So if I want to pursue some science, or engineering, or music, or writing, or math, and I want this activity to be part of my balanced job complex, the activity has to be regarded by the economy as worthy.

But how does the economy decide something is worthy? Most likely, for art as with engineering, by budgeting whole institutions that in turn incorporate people who do this type work, and by then respecting the employees' collective view as to the worthiness of pursuits undertaken.

Could it be that some genius will propose to a music workplace or an art workplace or a research center, pursuits that others feel deserve no time, energy, and resources, wrongly? Sure, it could happen. But parecon is far less vulnerable to such problems, having removed profit and power differentials from the motivations of all those involved, than is capitalism, say.

Ignorance may still have an impact leading to misperceptions, or just outright error, of course, in parecon as in any system at all. But, one can even try to account for the likely distribution of ignorance and try to guard against its having ill effects—which is just what elevating the value "diversity" to such a prime position in parecon is meant to help achieve (other techniques include things like tenure, etc.)

12. Seeking Participatory Allocation

Now the problem arises of how to unite freedom and organization; how to combine mastery of the workers over the work with the binding up of all this work in a well-planned social entirety. How to organize production, in every shop as well as over the whole of world economy, in such a way that they themselves as parts of a collaborating community regulate their work.
-Anton Pannekoek

Participatory planning is the allocation component of participatory economics. Producers and consumers organized in councils cooperatively negotiate labor, resource, and output allocations. The procedure organizes economic choices and simultaneously fosters participatory self-management. Production and consumption come into accord via a cooperative give and take among individuals and their councils, in which actors have proper influence and benefit in unison with (rather than in opposition to) one another. That's the vision, but visions result from long years of organizing, educating, and fighting for short-range demands that embody the vision's basic principles and that bring us incrementally closer to their realization, eventually amassing enough gains in consciousness, militancy, and organization to win the whole sought-after alteration,

So what short-run demands can foster participatory planning? Eight broad areas of change stand out.

Council Infrastructure and Knowledge Base

His name was George F. Babbitt, and ...
he was nimble in the calling of selling houses
for more than people could afford to pay.
-Sinclair Lewis

Participatory planning stands on two primary pillars: democratic participatory councils and wide dispersal of all information relevant to economic decision-making. Thus, to establish or strengthen workplace or consumer councils or to enlarge access of all producers and consumers to relevant information is to support participatory planning. For example, efforts to win workers' rights to meet and/or convene their own on-the-job, rank-and-file organizations are very positive. And likewise efforts to "open the books" in a firm or in government economic institutions are also part and parcel of developing norms and consciousness conducive to participatory planning.

Improved Pricing via taxation and subsidies

A touch of dishonesty is part of the very existence of private
merchandising. When a peasant buys a horse, he runs it
down in every possible way. If he sells the same horse
a year later, it will have become younger, better, and
stronger... One's own commodity will always be the
best-the other person's the worst. Deprecation of one's
competitors-a deprecation that is usually devoid
of all honesty-is an essential tool of one's business.
-Wilhelm Reich

One reason to favor participatory planning is that it gets prices right. Rather than over-valuing goods with negative public effects or under-valuing those with positive public effects, parecon properly accounts for impacts "external to the buyer and seller" by specifically accounting for the full social impact on all workers and consumers and on the environment.

So to intervene in markets to move prices toward true valuations is to promote participatory planning. For example, demands to tax goods with bad environmental or human by-products such as cars, liquor, or cigarettes, or to subsidize goods with desirable impact external to the "buyer and seller," such as health care, parks, low-income housing, and education, are all "pareconish."

Qualitative Descriptive Information

> *The trouble with the rat race is even if*
> *you win, you find out you're still a rat.*
> *-Lily Tomlin*

One of the methods parecon employs to ensure that its indicative prices reflect true social costs and benefits as well as guard against alienated behavior and mechanistic ignorance of the human dimensions of economics, is to incorporate into planning not only quantitative indicators, but also qualitative information about what goes into producing goods and what their consumption means to people.

It follows that demands about honest and comprehensive labeling and advertising, particularly to include information bearing on the conditions of workers or impact on broader social relations, can also foster the values and mindsets of parecon, contributing to preparing for its full implementation. Imagine honest labeling and advertising—truly honest labeling and advertising...

Sharing and Solidarity

> *While there is a lower class, I am in it.*
> *While there is a criminal element, I am of it.*
> *While there is a soul in prison, I am not free.*
> *- Eugene Debs*

One of the ills of market exchange is that it presses all actors toward individualist rather than collective consumption, even when this is harmful not only socially but to the direct participant. Parecon, in contrast, is as able to offer collective as private solutions. For example, are private autos better than decent public transit for inner city travel? On a smaller scale, does it make sense for everyone in an apartment complex to be almost totally isolated from everyone else, getting no benefits from sharing collective goods? Does it make sense to pay for the tremendous redundancy of everyone having their own instance of every imaginable commodity?

Workers' councils aren't the only place where citizens can usefully conceive and fight for worthy demands. Not only can consumer movements fight about prices and the provision of qualitative information, as indicated above, and about government budgets and related matters, as indicated below, they can also locally conceive how their members might benefit from pooling their resources and sharing purchases collectively. This kind of thing already happens, in fledgling form, in consumers' cooperatives, of course. The only struggle in this instance is with old mindsets but the resulting increase in social interaction, fulfillment, and solidarity is certainly part of building a pareconish mentality.

Human Needs not Profitability

> *I confess that I am not charmed with the ideal of life held out by those who think that the normal state of human beings is that of struggling to get on; that the trampling, crushing, elbowing, and treading on each other's heels, which form the existing type of social life, are the most desirable lot of human beings.*
> *-John Stuart Mill*

In parecon, unlike capitalism, collective consumption and investment are handled within the general planning process that gives each person proportionate input. This leads to collective consumption and investment interactively oriented toward the well-being and development of all actors. Thus, demands which seek to put people above profit in government economic choices are pareconish, whether we are talking about reducing war spending and curtailing sops to corporate power, or expanding social spending on housing, health, welfare, education, social infrastructure, or art.

Democratize Budgets

> *How can a rational being be ennobled by*
> *anything that is not obtained by its own exertions?*
> *-Mary Wollstonecraft*

One way to affect government budgets is to agitate on behalf of better choices, as above. Another way is to alter the processes by which budgets are proposed and then decided on.

Demands that increase public involvement and empowerment, particularly via fledgling council structures that could grow into parecon institutions, can improve our lot in the present and also lay the groundwork for a preferred future. The demand isn't for input into an unimportant subset of the budget, of course, but into how options are proposed throughout the budget, and into making decisions about proposed options.

More Leisure, Less Labor

> *A society that gives to one class all the opportunities*
> *for leisure and to another all the burdens of*
> *work condemns both classes to spiritual sterility.*
> *-Lewis Mumford*

Markets intrinsically pressure actors to work longer hours and enjoy less leisure. Competition does this nasty job by generating strong incentives to overwork and ensuring that if a few people do raise their labor hours, all others in related endeavors must do so as well, lest they suffer irreparable losses. Think of current high-powered law firms to see how this occurs even against the desires of powerful people. The lawyers are pushed into endlessly raising their billable hours, taking on as many new clients as can be had, even beyond their own manic personalities and greed. If they relent, some other firm may become more powerful than they are, gobbling up market share, and the non-manic firm runs the risk not merely of having less income due to opting for more leisure (which its members would prefer), but of losing their firm and thus income entirely. Thus we see an upward spiral in work hours per week and a decline in vacation time even as people grouse about no longer having lives to lead. And this occurs despite increasing productivity that could sustain high output without excessive labor allotments. Comparing 1960 to 2000, we could have the same per capita output now, but work literally half as much, say a four-hour workday, or two weeks off every month, or a year on and then a year off, alternately over our lifetimes, for example.

Parecons generate no such pressure to expand work hours regardless of growing productivity. The choice of upping output without limit (not to mention with most people not sharing in the enlarged product) or of having a life, is not biased to the former by continual fear of being out-competed.

Thus, demands over workday length, length of the work week, vacation time, and time more generally are not only good ways to redistribute wealth, they are also means to get at this leisure-destroying feature of our economy, and to propel pareconish calculations and aspirations.

Participatory Allocation in our Movements

It all depends, as you see, on what your purpose is, what you want to accomplish. Your aims determine the means. Means and aims are in reality the same: you cannot separate them. It is the means that shape your ends. The means are the

seeds which bud into flower and come to fruition. The fruit
will always be of the nature of the seed you planted.
You can't grow a rose from a cactus seed. No more can you
harvest liberty from compulsion, justice from dictatorship.
                                        -Alexander Berkman

As with every dimension of economic or other focus of movement struggle, it is necessary to incorporate in our own efforts
the aims and structures we propose for the broader society
outside. What can that mean in this case?

There is no allocation in each movement project and organization other than what we have mentioned in earlier chapters regarding remuneration or allocation of tasks. But what
about allocation among our projects and organizations? What
currently determines how many resources go to left print versus left radio versus left video, or to particular efforts in any of
these left media? What determines how many resources are at
the disposal of struggles around police violence and matters of
race, or reproductive rights and matters of gender, or international relations and matters of war and peace, or domestic or
global economics and matters of class? And what about allocations for local as compared to regional or national projects?

In the broad progressive or left community there is often
no self-conscious "allocation planning" of any sort at all, much
less any participatory planning. Allocation issues most often
aren't even openly raised, much less democratically decided.
In fact, a key determinant of current left allocation is competitive fund raising and essentially market- and power-defined
dynamics. But just as having a parecon movement implies
that within each institution we should seek balanced job complexes, just rewards in accord with effort and sacrifice, and
participatory self-management, shouldn't it also mean that
we attempt to imbue the left project as a whole with elements
of mutual aid and sharing and social planning?

As with other internal innovations, incorporating participatory allocation features in our movements won't be easy,
nor will it be accomplished overnight. After all, at the moment
progressive and left operations, projects, organizations, and

"businesses" are barely more entwined and socially planned than are their corporate counterpart institutions in the mainstream. At a minimum, then, without prejudging precisely what can and ought to be done, it seems fair to at least suggest that there is considerable room for innovation and improvement regarding movement "planning" and mutual benefit.

13. Economics and the Rest Of Society

What is it then makes people happy? Free and full life and the consciousness of life. Or, if you will, the pleasurable exercise of our energies and the enjoyment of the rest which that exercise or expenditure of energy makes necessary to us. I think that is happiness for all, and covers all the difference of capacity from the most energetic to the laziest. Now whatever interferes with that freedom and fullness of life, under whatever species guise it may come, is an evil; is some thing to be got rid of as speedily as possible. It ought not to be endured by reasonable men [and women], who naturally wish to be happy.
-William Morris

A participatory economy produces, consumes, and allocates to meet people's needs and develop their capacities. It also promotes equity, solidarity, diversity, and self- management. Its central features are workers' and consumers' councils, remuneration according to effort and sacrifice, balanced job complexes, and participatory planning. Yet, however high we may rate a parecon economically, a good society needs more than just a good economy.

Gender and the General Issues

Women will not simply be mainstreamed into the polluted stream. Women are changing the stream,

making it clean and green and safe for all—every
gender, race, creed, sexual orientation, age, and ability.
-Bella Abzug

Imagine a society with a participatory economy but sexist kinship institutions that subordinate women to men. What happens?

Parecon economic structures would violate a sexist household hierarchy by not subordinating women to men and by giving women and men expectations contrary to male supremacy. Sexist kinship arrangements would violate balanced job complexes by apportioning tasks unfairly in the home and by giving women and men expectations contrary to universal equity. The parecon would produce equitable expectations that the kinship sphere would violate. The kinship sphere would impart expectations of female subordination that the parecon economy would violate. But if an economy produces people who don't fit their households and households also socialize people who don't fit their economy, turmoil will follow and the economy or the households must change.

In light of this, suppose a feminist movement favors genderless parenting instead of mothering and fathering. Or maybe it rejects patriarchal marriage and the nuclear family. Whatever its preferences may be, a new feminist vision would certainly require that a compatible economy not violate kinship values. Likewise, a compatible kinship vision would have to respect parecon's economic requirements.

Once we understand this reciprocity, we see that building a participatory economy impacts building a feminist kinship sphere and vice versa, so the two efforts need to be accommodated or even made to enhance one another's logic. And similarly, for a good economy to fit with desired innovations in education, or the state, or culture, or international relations, it must incorporate structures that respect the new aims of those other realms—and vice versa. This is the logic of "economics and the rest of society" and here are some further indicative examples.

Education

> *This crippling of individuals I consider the worst*
> *evil of capitalism. Our whole educational system*
> *suffers from this evil. An exaggerated competitive*
> *attitude is inculcated into the student, who is trained to*
> *worship acquisitive success as a preparation for his future.*
> *- Albert Einstein*

Consider these two perceptions of the role of education:

1) Education should convey information and skills suited
to each individual meeting their own agendas. "Be the
best you desire to be."

2) Education should convey information and skills suited
to people filling available roles in the society. "Be what
society needs you to be."

For ideal educational institutions, we would want these
two aims to be mutually consistent and supportive. In a good
society, education for people to be what they desire should be
precisely what's needed to also prepare people for positions
that the society will willingly remunerate. In a good society,
education that prepares people to fit the society's roles should
also be education that furthers people's fulfillment and development. A good society, in other words, will offer people diverse role options that are in tune with and extrapolate from
their true desires and inclinations.

Capitalism's institutions, however, need from most people
regardless of their natural desires and inclinations, compli-
ance, passivity, and a willingness to obey orders and endure
boredom. Thus capitalism violates education for human fulfillment and development. Capitalist schools dumb most people down rather than preparing them to be the best they
desire to be. Parecon, in contrast, needs schools that educate
people to deal well with information, to make reasoned and informed decisions, and to utilize their special talents and ca-

pacities as they prefer. Parecon not only doesn't conflict with good educational priorities, it fosters them.

Race

The world is big. some people are unable to comprehend that simple fact. they want the world on their own terms, its peoples just like them and their friends, its places like the manicured patch on which they live. but this is a foolish and blind wish. Diversity is not an abnormality, but the very reality of our planet. The human world manifests the same reality and will not seek our permission to celebrate itself in the magnificence of its endless varieties. Civility is a sensible attribute in this kind of world we have; narrowness of heart and mind is not.
- Chinua Achebe

What a parecon imposes on race relations is that they not elevate one race above another regarding decision-making expectations or inclinations, income, or wealth. The parecon will violate racist inclinations in the economy, and compatibility will preclude them elsewhere. This, of course, is to the good.

In reverse, we can imagine that a good society would welcome great racial and cultural diversity—ethnic, religious, regional...whatever—providing space for each to pursue its own approaches to celebration, linguistic usage, interpersonal identification, and so on, so long as each operates consistent with the norm that their choices should not impede any other community's having equal freedom in its cultural pursuits.

Does this entail implications for the economy? It certainly could. For example, there is a question of working on holidays, or perhaps having the room at work to engage in certain practices that are culturally quite welcome and don't impinge on others, and so on. A participatory economy, celebrating diversity, would have no problem with such externally generated desires so long as they not impinge basic defining features such as dignified work or just rewards for all.

Ecology

> *The private ownership of the planet by elite strata must be brought to an end if we are to survive the afflictions it has imposed on the biotic world, particularly as a result of a society structured around limitless growth. Free nature, in my view, can only begin to emerge when we live in a fully participatory society literally free of privilege and domination. Only then will we be able to rid ourselves of the idea of dominating nature and fulfill our promise for acting as a moral, rational, and creative force in natural as well social evolution.*
> —*Murray Bookchin*

The relationship between parecon and the environment is subtle. Any economy says about addressing ecology, "fine, but do it consistently with business as usual." A market system thus says to those concerned about ecology, "fine, worry about ecology, but don't distort ecologically unsound market prices, or curtail ecologically unconcerned market transactions, or otherwise disrupt ecologically dismissive market logic."

In contrast, participatory planning properly values resources and ecological diversity in terms of their impact on human well-being and development. Pollution and unsustainable implications of all kinds, are accounted for by the intrinsic operations of a parecon. But beyond this structural aspect, some people might also value various species or even natural formations independent of the implications valuing these has for humans. And in response, a parecon can accommodate rules about impact on other species, but it will do so only if compelled to by outside constraints.

By its intrinsic logic, that is, a parecon values economic choices in terms of their implications for humans. It automatically accounts (as well as existing knowledge permits) for resource depletion or pollution or extinction effects or other ecological outcomes, insofar as these in turn impact human well-being and development. Additionally, in response to an

external advisory, a parecon can also avoid displacing or killing rhinos, snail darters, smallpox bacteria, or anything
else—even if displacing or killing rhinos, snail darters, smallpox bacteria, or anything else would benefit humans. In other
words, when society deems an extra-economic ecological con-
straint desirable, its imposition on a participatory economy
will not disrupt the economy's logic or efficiency.

But what about influences in the opposite direction? How
does a parecon impact people's independent ecological concerns and sensibilities? First, a parecon communicates to people focusing on ecology a strong impetus not to ignore the
human dimension. Indeed, it literally compels all actors, including those who are primarily motivated by ecological priorities, to account for the human implications of their economic
choices. And second, a parecon requires that ecological goals
be realized without compromising balanced job complexes, remuneration according to effort and sacrifice, council self-
management, and participatory planning—in effect, it says to
those concerned about sustainability, these are components of
sustainability too.

The State

> *What do you suppose will satisfy the soul*
> *except to walk free and own no superior.*
> *-Walt Whitman*

One implication of parecon for the state is that political functions will be enacted in balanced job complexes and be remunerated only for effort and sacrifice. For any vision of
adjudication, legislation, and political implementation, this
means that whatever political values we seek, they must not
violate pareconish economic values. Thus we won't have politics elevating some people to disproportionate power, rewarding some with unbalanced job complexes, or giving some
unjust income. Nor will the ideological or behavioral implica-

tions of political institutions obstruct producing and consuming in a pareconish way.

The legal system of a society is one typical political component we might consider. Currently in the U.S., attorneys for opposed parties do whatever they can get away with to win. Neither is primarily seeking truth or justice, yet truth and justice are supposed to emerge from their competition. This may remind us of the even more ridiculous but quite similar idea that economic buyers and sellers, each being greedy anti-social individualists, will maximally promote just economic outcomes. In any event, I suspect that a serious political vision won't dispense with adjudication or policing but will, instead, define these functions more sensibly and find ways to accomplish them that also meet broader political, economic, and social priorities. Do we get rid of police or court trials and have everyone in the society do whatever policing is called for and resolve their disputes only informally or locally? I doubt it. I suspect we will instead recognize that like piloting planes, or doing medical operations, or handling a big crane, some folks being specially trained in police and courtroom functions with other folks not having to prepare for or worry about these particular tasks, will yield better skills and better utilize them than having everyone do these tasks without specialization, not to mention that the former approach enhances diversity. But however we come to understand police and courtroom or other political responsibilities, if we also favor parecon, we will require balanced job complexes and participatory self-management for those doing them, of course.

International Relations

Capitalism is the astounding belief that
the most wickedest of men will do the most
wickedest of things for the greatest good of everyone.
-John Maynard Keynes

If we aspire to a parecon nationally, the consistent international economic goal seems pretty obvious. Why should a child born in a country with fewer resources or with a history of being dominated by colonialism have a worse life than a child born in a resource-rich country or a country that has colonially exploited others for decades? People born in different parts of the world should not suffer (or benefit) due to accidents of geography or past history. Thus a particular society with a parecon should deal with other nations in ways that reduce unjust differences in average income and circumstance as rapidly as possible without disrupting lives so much as to do more harm than good.

That said, there is nothing in the structure of a participatory economy per se that militates toward one or another approach to other countries, other than, of course, the way in which each parecon produces in its populace a sense of generalized solidarity and justice. Still, we might expect that a minimal but important step would be that in trading with other countries not yet parecon in structure, a participatory economy would favor whichever price—the international market price or the parecon valuation within the parecon society—that most benefitted the worse-off trade partner. Beyond this, it could offer various forms of aid, etc.

Thus, if a pareconish U.S. is entering into a trade relation with some other poorer country and the international market price for the good is $10 per unit, but the U.S. parecon indicative price for the good is $13 per unit, when the country says you can have what you request for $10 million, the U.S. says, thank you but here is $13 million—and, we would hope, says as well, here is aid, tools, equipment, etc. to redress differentials that have no moral or economic reason for persisting.

Other questions arise. How much of their living standards can we expect—or should we hope—people in much wealthier societies would give up when doing so can be translated into improvements in circumstances for those worse off around the world? And thus how much aid would they decide to offer, subtracting from domestic innovation and consumption to make it possible? Well, who knows? Different people will have different views on this matter, as on most others, of course. Parecon is a vision for an economy and doesn't prejudge what is consumed, how much is allotted for investment, or how much is allotted for international aid. On the other hand, insofar as countries join the international community of parecons, there is presumably great pressure to steadily equilibrate incomes and conditions so that across all countries the values of solidarity, diversity, self-management, and equity are steadily pursued and attained.

The Bottom Line

We are at war, and that war is not simply a hot debate between the capitalist camp and the socialist camp over which economic/political/social arrangement will have hegemony in the world. It's not just the battle over turf and who has the right to utilize resources for whomsover's benfit. The war is also being fought over the truth: what is the truth about human nature, about the human potential?
- Toni Cade Bambara

*Let me say, with the risk of appearing ridiculous, that the true revolutionary is guided by strong feelings of love. It is impossible to think of an authentic revolutionary without this quality. This is perhaps one of the greatest dramas of a leader, [to] combine an impassioned spirit with a cold mind and make painful decisions without flinching one muscle...
In these conditions one must have a large dose of humanity, a large dose of a sense of justice and truth, to avoid falling into dogmatic extremes, avoid falling into cold scholasticism, into isolation from the masses...
Above all, always be capable of feeling any injustice committed against anyone anywhere in the world. That is the most beautiful quality of a revolutionary.*
-Che Guevara

Obviously the above discussion is limited. Yet, nonetheless, many readers will easily agree that a good society should have equity of circumstance and income between men and women, respect for diversity of sexual and social choices, freedom for cultural communities to exist without fear of penalty and a general social respect for diversity, full political participation and full dissemination of information and skills essential to universal participatory self-management, respect for the natural environment as it affects humanity and also in its own right, and a steady equalization of wealth and circumstances internationally. But I suspect many readers would also easily agree that to answer the question "what do you want" and sufficiently to inform our strategic choices, we need more detailed and convincing descriptions of positive cultural, kinship, political, ecological, and international values and institutions.

The limited point of this chapter, therefore, is that if these new visions are to be compatible with parecon, they must not abrogate and ideally will even help promote parecon's economic priorities and norms. Likewise, if parecon is to be compatible with these necessary new visions, parecon's economic implications must not abrogate and ideally will even help promote their kinship, sexual, cultural, political, ecological, and international priorities and norms.

14. Q&A: Economics and Society

If we do not now dare everything,
the fulfillment of that prophesy,
recreated from the bible in
song by a slave, is upon us:
God gave Noah the rainbow sign,
no more water, the fire next time!
-James Baldwin

Women's Work, or "Other Labor"

- *How would parecon reward "secondary labor" that women the world over are responsible for: the bearing and rearing of children, and the making of "home" or household?*

If household functions were deemed work in a parecon as Wages for Housework advocates might prefer, then they would be part of the planning process, allocated in balanced job complexes. All questions of equity, control, diversity, solidarity, etc. would be handled as with any other kind of work.

On the other hand, if household functions were deemed, let's say, kinship activity, and not part of the economy per se in a society with a parecon, then the determination of how they are done and in what relationships would depend on the values and structures of the kinship sphere of life (as opposed to the economy).

However, just as the economy has to be compatible with the cultural/community sphere of life, the polity, and kinship, so vice versa. Thus, if kinship says male and female have very limited implications for life choice and human capability and inclination, the economy cannot have a sexual division of labor. And if the economy says people must respect equity of circumstance and empowerment, the kinship sphere cannot allocate its kinship activities in a non-equitable fashion re fulfillment or empowerment. Thus, if rearing children, etc., is not deemed first and foremost economic activity, still in a parecon it will have to be handled equitably if the kinship sphere and the economy are to be compatible.

- *The system you've designed doesn't account for the fact that women are already under represented at work. Moving them into a participatory scheme would necessitate a radical restructuring of childcare and home work as a prerequisite to their equal participation. How do you resolve this?*

It isn't that the parecon system doesn't account for current conditions of child care and home work, it is that a visionary model isn't a description or plan for how to attain and create the vision. It is just about the established good economy.

If home work and child care isn't deemed economic, then everyone has to do a full share of economic work, in a balanced job complex. The home and childcare work would have to be equally shared or women would be exhausted, as now in many instances. But it wouldn't have to be planned in the same fashion as production in typical workplaces. It would be, instead, a part of consumption or other dimensions of social life.

On the other hand, if homework and childcare is part of the economy, then the dictates of parecon guarantee equitable and just allocations for men and women, and for all those involved. In any event, I agree with you that a parecon requires a different kinship sphere than we now have—one that doesn't produce patriarchy, for example, or commercial class attitudes either.

- *But isn't it true that to move women into a participatory system, you would have to move childcare and home-based work into the parecon system, to free up enough time for them to begin to participate?*

This I don't quite follow. It is one way to proceed but by saying that it is the only way, it seems to assume that however much child care and home-based work occurs, it must inevitably occupy women more. Why is that? It seems much more likely to me that it will be shared, handled collectively, in various kinds of new living arrangements. Indeed, it seems to me that our vision for kinship relations will probably require this for reasons that have to do with eliminating hierarchies of power and other unjust phenomena among men and women, not simply for the reasons that a parecon would require it.

There is also a good case to be made that home-based work is a rather private and personal affair, the volume of which is to a considerable extent a matter of one's own choosing, not subject to an economic plan, and the output of which is for oneself, not for others in the economy. This is what makes consideration of it a bit complex.

For example, suppose you and another person live together and opt for a very fancy house arrangement that takes a whole lot of work because you like the elaborate layout and floor plan and floral arrangements and whatnot, which entails all this work. Should all the work that you do on this stuff count toward your economic contribution to society and should all the inputs not go against your incomes, even though you and your partner are virtually the only beneficiaries of the excess household labors? It may well be more just, in fact, to say that we are all responsible for our own living arrangements, cleanliness, and so on, using our incomes and energies as we choose, in addition to whatever is the average workload that society has settled on for the economy (presumably much reduced from now). That seems preferable to me, at any rate. But I think good values and insights on these issues depend, in considerable degree, on a powerful, compelling, and liberatory vision for kinship institutions in general—which is why we don't get into it too much when discussing parecon as an economy, feeling we don't have the insight to do so.

Government and Parecon

- *Would a government exist in parecon separate from the economy?*

What we call political institutions today—local, state and national governments—actually perform both political and economic functions. This is because our present economy consists of a market system, and markets will lead to the production of few if any public goods, and because there are certain public goods whose non-production is so unacceptable that every market economy has got to substitute some other decision-making mechanism for the market mechanism regarding these public goods. In our economy local, state, and national governments therefore have to double as economic institutions for the purchase of minimal amounts of certain public goods—for which they collect taxes.

But as much as the economic decisions of today's "political" institutions dominate their time and our interest in them, they do debate and decide other more "political" things as well, like war and peace, whether drugs are legal or not, what the rules and procedures of the criminal justice system will be, whether America the Beautiful or the Star Spangled Banner will be the national anthem, immigration policy, etc. My ideas about what kinds of political institutions and procedures would be best for making these kinds of political decisions run along democratic, participatory lines. What are the most desirable political institutions and why? How should we accomplish political functions such as legislation, adjudication, and implementation in ways that not only achieve our political aims, but also further values we hold dear such as solidarity, equity, self management, and diversity? These are really the same questions as led to developing parecon economic institutions, only transposed to the political realm.

Is "no state" a slogan that captures what is needed? I don't honestly think so, though I respect the anti-authoritarian impetus. Of course we want no authoritarian state, no apparatus that is above and separate from the populace, imposing outcomes on the populace against our own interests and desires. But that doesn't mean that all political functions just disappear. Saying we want no state may have some subtle meaning for a few folks, but to most it sounds like saying we want no polity. It conflates bad political institutions with all political institutions, saying that we don't want the former but sounding like we don't want the latter. Saying we don't want a state, meaning (or even just being taken to mean) we don't want any kind of political institutions, is like saying for the economy, we can do without it, we can have everyone produce and consume whatever they want, as if there are no complicated issues that require institutions and thus serious thought about the structure of those institutions. We cannot forego political institutions but instead need a political vision with specifically political institutions to accomplish political functions in ways we desire, just as we need an economic vision with economic institutions to accomplish economic functions desirably.

Ecology and Parecon

- *How would natural resource and pollution management work under a parecon? Take trees, for example. I assume that legislation would need to be passed saying that the economy as a whole can cut down so many trees a year (a sustainable number), as long as they are replanted, etc.*

Perhaps, perhaps not. Take instead for a minute some animal with no relevance whatever for human well being and development. Say a species that people don't see, interact with, or get anything from, as far as anyone knows. Suppose this species, in part, exists in places where humans might clear land for use. If society wants to preserve the species it would need to pass a law, as you say, imposing restraints on the economy which might otherwise just wipe the species out. The point is, economic calculation of true and complete human and social costs and benefits wouldn't even include reference to this particular species so unless there was a law protecting it, there would be no gainsay it wouldn't be wiped out.

But the logging case is different. The trees do have great value, one presumes, for human well being and development, and so the cost of their use climbs immensely as they are treated in a manner that would make them irreplaceable. So, the economy actually prices the trees to take into account true social costs and benefits associated with using them...as best it can. Whether you would need rules on top of that or not isn't clear. I doubt it, but it could be done, no problem.

- *But with such laws would the indicative price then rise until the workplaces harvesting trees weren't asking for more than were available?*

Go back to the peculiar species. The law preventing its decimation wouldn't cause the social costs of clearing the land it lived on to go up and therefore wouldn't affect the indicative price. Economic actors might want to do it, as they rightly should, being motivated by human well-being and development. The law would simply prevent their doing it. In the case that you describe, the economic system would rightly perceive the social cost implications of the cutting. An additional law wouldn't be needed, unlike the species case above.

Now, let's say that consumers want all these wooden products, and are not discouraged by the high price. They can't all have them. How would this conflict be resolved?

I think you may be asking two questions. First, if the price doesn't stop the clear-cutting, but the society wants it stopped, then what? A law. Second, if something is scarce, who gets it? First come first served, presumably. This can happen, as well, when something innovative takes off. Suppose people's plans say so much of item "a" is needed in the economy for this year, and the third month into the planned year something happens that makes item "a" much more desirable and many more people want it, so the firm producing it can't keep up. Well, there are adjustments that would increase output, but perhaps much less than demand, for some items. Then not everyone who wants it now (wants to change their consumption request for this item), and can afford it now, gets it now. Why? Because the price doesn't climb to preclude buyers. This is also a phenomenon in centrally planned economies and is why there are queues there rather than rising prices which reduce the length of the line until there are only as many people as items to be had.

- *Can you also explain how setting pollution controls might work under a parecon? Are the levels set for the economy as a whole? What if I don't want any pollution in my neighborhood? Do I have to resort to legal means to stop workplace Y from polluting there, or are there economic means at my disposal?*

Pollution is part of what is counted into the social costs and benefits associated with production and consumption. So the price of products reflects the pollution—and the cost of cleaning it up. For example, suppose a plant produces something for a national audience, and, given the social costs and benefits there is a lot of demand for it. And suppose pollution leaves the plant and congregates above a local community, primarily affecting its citizens.

Now what?

What is the just approach? It isn't automatic. It involves assessment of social costs and benefits, and available options. Suppose it is a relatively unimportant product and the local environmental effect is devastating. Then, by the principle that those affected have a say proportional to the effect on them, the price should climb much higher, due to the high effect on the community, not to mention the potential buyers, who wouldn't want the relatively minor product, priced out of desirability. The same plant located somewhere where the human impact of the pollution is nil, however, might be fine.

Suppose instead the product is absolutely critical and there is no way to have the plant be anywhere else for the coming year. Now what? Well, maybe the community of people needs to be moved, if it is suffering that greatly—or protected somehow. But the plant continues.

Now what kind of economic system can measure the desires and benefits and negative and positive impacts of production and consumption so as to provide indicative prices reflecting them properly, and so as to levy fees so that such clean-ups and the like can be done humanely. Parecon is, I believe, the answer.

In Neoclassical economics there is a whole subdivision of analysts that tries to figure out how you modify markets to address such matters. Some of these folks are just tinkering in the interests of capital. But some take the problem seriously, albeit accepting markets as inevitable. When you take their quite technical answers and you recognize the ubiquity of external effects (which they don't) you get a pattern of alterations and reforms, which, quite interestingly, leads rather inexorably to an inefficient and clumsy version of what parecon does rather smoothly. Take a look at the South End Press or Princeton University Press books on the topic—*Looking Forward* or *The Political Economy of Participatory Economics*—if your interest is that great, for how the production units are charged for their costs of production, including pollution clean-up, etc. The logic is here, the details are there.

Trade

- *How would international trade work in and among parecons? What reason would there be for a national parecon of, say, British Columbia and Alberta (combined), which would be self-sufficient in almost everything, to give oil to primarily agricultural areas like Saskatchewan and Manitoba?*

Think of two parecon societies. What is the relevant "index" difference if we were to compare? Well, regarding the economy—there may be many non-economic differences, of course—the first thing to look at would be the balanced job complexes in each society. Is one superior in its qualities to the other? The second thing would be the per-capita consumption bundle. Is one better than the other? In assessing this, of course, one has to include how long people work.

There is no moral justification I can think of for one country having better circumstances than another, so I think a pareconish attitude in this realm is to have exchange rates, which, over time, facilitate equalization. There are many ways to envision trading between two such countries, even in accord with this norm (which could be pursued more or less quickly) or between either and a non-parecon country, for that matter.

Two parecon countries could, in essence, treat each other as large units in a single larger economic entity. They could, alternatively, be quite independent and trade items with the valuations being that of either one country or the other, or set by some agreed standard, or according to the international rate of exchange, for that matter. The rule could be—I like this one—that such trade occurs at valuations of the country whose valuations yield better outcomes for the economy that is less developed. A similar rule could exist for trade with non-parecons. Thus, the parecon trades at the going international exchange rates, or at the prices of the trade partner, or at its own indicative prices, whichever benefits the nonparecon economy.

- *Would there be structural incentives for these two areas to amalgamate, or would the West see the prairies as just millions more consumers with nothing much to add to the West's standard of living?*

This is one problem of parecon, I suppose. If you draw the border around a rich region, then it will have high incomes and wonderful job complexes. A poor region will be the opposite.

The commitment to equalize life conditions and opportunities is just that, a commitment, not a structural imperative, even with parecon. There is no system I know of that does better, however. Maybe someone can come up with one. I don't know anything about the areas you mention, and can't even hazard a guess.

15. Participatory Economic Program

...would you tell me please
which way we should go from here? [Alice]
That depends a good deal
on where you want to get to. [The Cat]
-Lewis Carroll

It is necessary with bold spirit and in good conscience
to save civilization.... We must halt the dissolution
that corrupts the roots of human society. The bare and
barren tree can be made green again. Are we not ready?
-Antonio Gramsci

Participatory economics is a set of institutions for accomplishing production, consumption, and allocation while meeting people's needs and furthering their development; a set of institutions designed to propel equity, solidarity, diversity, and self-management; a set of institutions centered upon democratic councils, remuneration according to effort and sacrifice, balanced job complexes, and participatory planning; a set of institutions that answers the question: if not capitalism, what do you want?

Participatory economic program is a set of demands meant to win improvements in people's lives in the short run while laying the basis for more gains and eventually winning a participatory economy in the long run. It includes demands for...

- Just rewards—including profit, wealth, inheritance, luxury, and income taxes, affirmative action, full employment, minimum wage supports, social wage supports, reverse income taxes, higher wages, and also just rewards inside our movements.

- Self-management—including workers' and consumers' councils, democratized information access, democratized workplace decision-making, consumer power over production norms, democratized budgets, and also self-management inside our own movements.

- Dignified work—including upgrading degrading jobs, regulating overly empowering jobs, creating balanced jobs, empowering all workers, and also dignifying and balancing work in our own movements.

- Participatory planning—including fostering council infrastructure and democratic knowledge disbursement, social regulation of prices, expansion of qualitative descriptive information, enlargement of solidarity, placing human needs above profitability, democratizing budgets, and winning more leisure and less labor. Participatory planning also envisions participatory allocation inside our movements, and democratized and just international relations including abolishing the World Bank, IMF, and WTO and instituting in their place democratic agencies subordinate to the will of local populations and seeking to regulate world trade and exchange to the benefit of the participants who are worst off.

All the above has been discussed in the foregoing chapters and now one final step concludes the argument.

Suppose we adopt a participatory program encompassing all the above. What do we then highlight as our central demand? What feature becomes the lynchpin of our efforts, the element that produces public visibility and widespread support? What is our version of "abolish slavery," "get the vote," "end the war," "free my people"? What current demand within the broad program can best:

- address needs that people currently feel
- propel parecon consciousness-raising
- empower people to seek still more gains, and
- galvanize people to win sought gains and simultaneously advance the encompassing broader program it is part of?

Parecon Program

> *The reasonable man adapts himself to the world;*
> *the unreasonable man persists in trying*
> *to adapt the world to himself. Therefore,*
> *all progress depends on the unreasonable man.*
> *- George Bernard Shaw*

I am going to hazard a guess about which demand might best encapsulate these goals...very loosely and broadly, and pending more evidence.

- We demand one quarter less work time for everyone, plus a parallel one quarter drop in wage and bonus income for the top quarter income earners in society (including an additional quarter profit tax on their income from capital), no change in total wage income for the middle half of society, and a one quarter raise in total wage income for the bottom quarter of society.

- We demand overtime must be paid at twice the rate of normal time and firms cannot hire or maintain overtime workers while there are applicants for normal time labor.

- We provide that anyone who wishes to work beyond three quarters of their current load can do so, but only in special employment programs initiated and paid by the government, administered locally by workers and consumers, and directed at improving local health care, education, social services, public housing, or other basic functions in poor communities where pay for this "surplus" work would be at twice the minimum wage (and the minimum wage, by the above requirements, would be two-thirds above what it was before this demand is won, until other pressures raise it still further).

• We demand the government invest in social programs including: training the unemployed to fill newly open work positions, training folks in previously unskilled jobs to take up higher skilled work left unattended by the reduction in workload of the currently well-employed, oversight of the whole system in each workplace by unions and workers' councils, the research and activism to pare away socially useless labor in advertising and similar worthless pursuits, and service work for those wanting to add their energies to advancing health care, education, social services, public housing, etc.

This work reduction and income-altering scenario releases—I think—more income than it hands out, assuming any resultant lost output is confined to useless and pointless products. But does the freed income (equal to one quarter of the current wages, bonuses, and profits of the top quarter income earners in society) fall short of the costs of the job program plus the costs of training? Perhaps, and if so, we then demand that the government reduce defense spending and spending on the prison industrial complex—and thereby free appropriate people to work in the real economy making up for lost hours and funds needed to handle program expenses.

What would all this do?

Well, by reducing everyone's work time commitments by 25% it would greatly empower the public to have time to develop agendas of change and to fight for them. People can do

this with their newfound time either through the social programs by which they can also get additional income, or via volunteer movement activism.

The demands would also dramatically redistribute income. Even before derivative impact on bargaining power
changes wages further, the top quarter earns wages at the
same rate as before, though losing a quarter of their profit income and of course a quarter of their wages and bonuses due
to reduced labor time. Yet even this group can be addressed
about the benefits of the program not only in moral terms regarding the well being of others, but also because through the
changes they will get more free time and will also enjoy many
of the social benefits such as reduced hostility in society, increased public goods, and so on.

The next half of the population has a one-third hourly pay
rate increase so that they earn the same amount as before but
for three quarters the time spent at work. They therefore benefit from reduced work time, from an increased hourly pay
rate, from the social spending, and also from the changed balance of power between society's classes due to newfound secu-
rity, etc.

The bottom quarter of the population also spends three
quarters the time spent before at work (though the unemployed of course increase their time at work), but now they get
a quarter more total pay than before, which is a two thirds
hourly pay increase. They also benefit most from the new social spending and changes in the balance of power among society's classes.

Obviously the program immediately improves the condition of society's worst off, but, more, it diminishes and perhaps
even eliminates unemployment, thereby securing the weak
against job threats by the strong, further empowering workers to win still higher wages as they solidify their new
strength. The redirection of much labor to social programs
also not only benefits the poorest constituencies in society directly, due to new schools, housing, etc, it also greatly empow-
ers them, leading in turn to new demands for better wages
and conditions and other social improvements. Likewise, ef-

forts to replace highly skilled labor allotments reduced by a quarter for such jobs, uplifts other workers, eliminating barriers to entry to better tasks at work.

The supremely strategic aspect of the program is, I think, that at its heart is a core demand to work fewer hours, something that people at every level of our society think is warranted and desirable and which no one will be able to argue against powerfully. The rest of the program flows logically from the desire to reduce hours in ways most beneficial to the worst off while improving the overall quality of society, rather than enriching only the powerful and already privileged. In addition the program opens doors to issues of remuneration, power, job definition and allocation, and budgeting and broad valuations. The program, in other words, wins terrain that leaves folks not only immediately better off, but also more empowered and ready to struggle on.

When thinking about what might be a lynchpin of an economic campaign that would galvanize broad and deep support, I gravitated to demands about length of work time and associated income because my experiences suggest that time pressure is greatly felt, greatly despised, and a great barrier to radicalization...and therefore a great target for a massive campaign. The whole project just embellishes demanding thirty hours work for forty hours pay, and, I admit, even that simple demand, all by itself, even without the diverse pareconish caveats and improvements, would be a wonderful centerpiece for a parecon movement. Embellished more or less as above, however, seeking a quarter less work time looks to me like a wonderful lightning rod, lynchpin, and foundation for struggle.

16. Q&A: Getting There

If we are to consider ourselves revolutionaries, we must acknowledge that we have an obligation to succeed in pursuing revolution. Here, we must acknowledge not only the power of our enemies, but our own power as well. Realizing the nature of our power, we must not deny ourselves the exercise of the options available to us; we must utilize surprise, cunning and flexibility; we must use the strength of the enemy to undo him, keeping him confused and off-balance. We must organize with perfect clarity to be utterly unpredictable. When our enemies expect us to respond to provocation with violence, we must react calmly and peacefully; just as they anticipate our passivity, we must throw a grenade.
- Stokely Carmichael

• *Even if we win something like a parecon, won't there always be huge resistance from some people who preferred the old system, like Ross Perot, say?*

You ask, suppose most citizens decide in favor of parecon, or militate in favor of it, and we win this transformation. Some still won't want the change—in particular, rich people with lots of property. True enough. Indeed, capitalists will fight by any means they can usefully and self-servingly muster to prevent any new system that would take away their private property.

There is no parecon created in the U.S., say, alongside Ross Perot (the example you gave) still owning means of production. Creating a parecon means, among many other things, that the private holdings of economic infrastructure of the rich are taken from them...against their wills, no doubt, in most cases.

Over time, increasingly the workers in GM become advocates of a new type of economy, even while GM is still privately owned and pursuing profit. And during this period the GM workers battle for better conditions, new job definitions, and all manner of other positive steps. But, when the GM workers and all others seeking a new economy win, there is a large change. No longer are they fighting against a class of owners seeking profit, or a class of coordinators maximizing their own relative advantages. Now, the prior owners no longer own, and the coordinator class is no more.

- *How is this ever going to happen? The fact that the rich can buy a lot more guns, and even make other poor people fight for them pretty much explains the current situation and a lot of history.*

All historical progress, from the ending of feudalism and slavery through women's rights, the end of Jim Crow, inauguration of labor rights, and so on, is impossible if one cannot make progress against an initially richer and better armed opponent—but, of course, one can. This is what organizing and developing opposition movements is all about. But the main solution to the other side having lots of guns and being able to pay people to brandish them is to organize those people so they become unwilling to play such a rule. There is no such thing as out-shooting something like the U.S. army, or even its police forces, even if such a scenario wouldn't corrupt participants and have unacceptable casualties—which it would. What can be done instead is to build ever larger movements which incorporate ever more constituencies and use diverse tactics to essentially disarm elites by creating conditions in which elites cannot exploit what advantages they have, whether money, or communicative tools, or forces of repression, until finally winning the allegiance of their troops right out from under them.

- *It seems to me that the best way to try to achieve something like Participatory Economics is to first try to get society closer to the situation by small steps. Do you agree?*

The best approach is the approach that works. Most likely this will involve, in part, winning a variety of reforms that make the existing system less painful for most folks. But one can do that, and still not create a launch pad for real change, so to speak, falling back, later, when capital becomes resurgent. Sweden is an example. Or one can win the needed gains, and at the same time create an ever stronger movement, able to aim for and win still more, in a trajectory that continues until the new economy is in place. Each gain is a reform. The former is a reformist approach to them. The latter is a non-reformist approach.

- *It seems that parecon would be less efficient in the way that efficiency is defined now. I don't see how a socially responsible system could compete with one that doesn't concern itself with questions of pollution and oppression. However, if that is true, how can we ever expect the whole world to suddenly change?*

Parecon doesn't have to appear everywhere in the world all at once. While it is a system with a logic and with principles, and capitalism is a different system with a different logic and with different principles, and the logic and dynamics of each system are inconsistent with that of the other—and undermine the successful reproduction of the other system to the extent that they co-exist in the same time and space—parts of parecon can exist and grow in a hostile capitalist framework. In fact, that is exactly what will have to happen. It is part of what we should call "the transition from the economics of fear and greed, i.e. capitalism, to the economics of equitable cooperation, i.e. parecon" and should recognize as a really important and difficult question. Thus establishing institutions in the present that embody some or even many features of a parecon is desirable partly as a means of learning, partly for inspiration, partly to fill needs.

However, if a country adopted a parecon system, it could still trade and even borrow from or lend to countries using capitalist systems. With capitalist economies that were richer than the parecon, relations would be quite simple. Enter into trade and borrowing relations that benefit the parecon economy—and bargain, maneuver, push, pull, manipulate to get the best terms of trade and credit terms possible for the parecon—since getting more than the lion's share of the benefits of international economic relations for the poorer country is completely consistent with parecon principles.

If the other country is a poorer parecon economy, the trade and credit relations that are consistent with parecon principles would require the richer parecon economy to grant the poorer one more than half the benefits that result from the efficiency gain due to the trade or lending activity. If the other country is a poorer capitalist country, things are a little more complicated. Parecon principles would require that the parecon country NOT drive the hardest bargain it could get—and appropriate the lion's share of the benefits from trade and lending—but instead to make sure that the poorer economy, even though it is capitalist, benefited equally if not more from the trade or international lending arrangements.

The exception to this is if such actions helped stabilize the capitalist ruling class in the poorer capitalist country. Then the parecon country should let the anti-capitalist movement in the poorer capitalist country decide if the parecon economy should drive a hard bargain, drive a hard bargain and give the liberation movement the financial gain, or boycott in order to help the liberation movement overthrow capitalism. Exporting revolution and international solidarity are admittedly tricky, tricky issues. But these are political, not economic subtleties.

- *Have you considered that the risks of a drastic change in the system may be too great? Isn't incremental change towards a more principle-based economic system a better alternative?*

Well, what are the drastic things that change? Private owner-ship of means of production disappears. Production for profit or surplus and misspecification of exchange values disap-pears. Hierarchicalization of daily life economic functions dis-appears. And so on...

But these are all things that should disappear.

This is a goal. How we get to it is another question. It isn't going to be monopoly capital one day, and then parecon the next day, obviously.

There is one sense in which your question has a lot of weight, I think. One can seek changes in capitalism that do not bother capitalists much, or that even benefit them. These are easy to fight for and to win, relatively. One can fight for changes that reduce or even terminate the capitalist's advan-tages, but benefit coordinators, and these are much harder to win because capitalists oppose these and have many resources with which to fight them. One can fight for changes that not only reduce and eventually eliminate capitalist advantage, but also coordinator advantage—the parecon path.

Is the parecon path hardest? Well, it comes up against two-pronged instead of one-pronged opposition. At the same time, however, it will better galvanize and motivate allies of change—working people. So both sides are strengthened, po-tentially. The opponents of change move from primarily capi-talists to including many coordinator class members. But the advocates of change while losing some coordinators, gain far greater allegiance from workers. Will it be easier or harder, once it gets going? I don't know. But I do believe that devoting one's life to attaining changes which leave capitalists as a rul-ing class, or which leave coordinators as a ruling class (as in the old Soviet system, or Yugoslav system) doesn't gain enough in probability of successful and irreversible innova-tion to make it the preferred option.

In fact, my inclination is to think that pursuing the road to parecon is probably the fastest way to win the kinds of innova-tions that a seriously concerned, pro-worker activist should want to win.

- *The initial problem is to get enough people to commit to a parecon. Should we start by forming a consumer's council (in the spirit of a Nader-like consumer group, but with the goal of building a new economy)?*

I think there is nowhere in the country where anyone is anywhere near having a community that could function largely outside the market economy...because we don't have means of production, clearly. But establishing consumer councils that operate as much as they can along parecon-like norms, and, for that matter, councils in workplaces with similar agendas, or whole workplaces within the economy but utilizing parecon-like values and structures, are all, I think, worthwhile undertakings. But so is trying to win non-reformist reforms in existing structures.

That is, there are two broad ways to pursue a new type of economy—building infrastructure that teaches its characteristics and prepares for it by literally creating elements of it in the present, on the one hand, and pushing existing institutions toward it, on the other. Each approach, if it is to make progress, needs to address meeting current needs and desires. Each approach, if it is to avoid pitfalls, needs to be tightly connected to the other, I think. The experimental and exemplary institutions need to retain touch with the real lives of normal citizens and their struggles. The movements within existing institutions need to retain touch with efforts to define and refine longer term goals to inform these immediate struggles. The two way exchange of ideas, energy, resources, time, and whatever else proves possible, is essential.

- *It seems to me that the left is sorely lacking when it comes to talking about/supporting alternative business models. What do you think?*

Creating pareconish institutions is a very positive thing to do. They are schools for the future. They display the values we favor in real settings and are exemplary and hopefully inspiring in that sense, They will presumably do many tasks better than using mainstream structures, instead—and certainly the type of tasks we are generally trying to accomplish.

The same can be said, by the way, for trying to embody the aims/values we have for gender, race, and power in our efforts, though that is another matter.

But believing something is very valuable is not the same as thinking it is alone valuable. Yes, creating a bookstore,, food distribution center, publishing house, or production plant that embodies parecon values and structures is valuable. But so is organizing within existing institutions to make them (a) less painful to people and (b) more in tune with future aims.

If creating a pareconish project or co-op or is good on grounds that it is exemplary, that it educates, it trains, and it also liberates those involved, then surely all this can also be said for organizing a labor movement, for example, that begins to build council structures in existing workplaces and wins reforms that benefit folks and embody desired values.

- *In order to get parecon going I think you would have to have enough of the basic industries (food, fuel, etc...) such that the parecon economy would be somewhere close to self-sufficient. How can we ever get that far?*

This just isn't the way the world works. You can't even conceive that folks will in huge numbers separate from existing institutions and create counter ones, such that, for example, there is a sphere of food production and distribution that is pareconish next to one that is capitalist, and the former is comparable in size and scope to the latter.

Why? Well because long before you got anywhere near that stage there would be no capitalism. Parallel structures do not exist in isolation. If those are growing, it means the values of the new orientation are spreading, and that will be happening because there are movements fighting for changes and gains all over society, throughout its institutions, political, cultural, kinship, and economic. And long before half of the people working in various industries would pick up and leave them, they will, in effect, seize them.

More, what does one use for property and capital in these parallel ventures? If one is taking that, too, then that is an immense struggle and if one can win that struggle, well then one has long since achieved the capacity to, again, transform the existing institutions.

* *Half the economy parecon, half capitalist —that isn't going to happen. Isn't the capitalist side too powerful?*

The process by which parallel pareconish institutions grows is not some kind of isolated dynamic which occurs off by itself. It impacts and is fed by what is happening throughout society.

A more accurate formulation, I think, would be that a movement which attempted to transform (in this case) the economy, more or less by stealth—that is, by simply building a whole new one step by step while not contesting inside the old one, would be totally doomed and misconceived. It just doesn't have anything to do with reality. It would have no means of gaining the resources, no means to defend against incursions—and, much more to the point, it would not have a process for recruiting support and participation.

On the other hand, if efforts to create parallel institutions are tied to and very aggressively support efforts within existing institutions to win changes there, that is another story. But in that case, long before the independent parallel institutions were so huge, we would have won.

Now, suppose we think of parallel institutions a bit more flexibly, a bit more in tune with what is in fact possible on a massive scale. Thus, we think of the formation of a worker's council in a plant and in an industry as a parallel institution, just as much as we think of a pareconish publishing house or food center as one.

Now we are getting more real. We have these parallel efforts and projects and structures which take many forms in many venues and which are able to reach out to the whole population and to be entered by that population without enormous dislocation. And if those parallel structures (whether the publishing houses or the food coops or the councils inside workplaces, or, for that matter, the neighborhood or regional consumer councils, or whatever) in turn also support efforts to win valuable changes in the mainstream—changes which improve people's conditions and lives and which also empower people (and those dissident structures, too), we are on to something valuable, I agree.

- *What are the impediments to building pareconish institutions?*

There are many. People with training and talent can often earn much more by following other paths. The near impossibility of getting financing impedes purchasing needed infrastructure.

You might like to try, some time, going to a bank for a loan if you are from a pareconish institution...it isn't a very lucrative way to spend one's time. On the other hand, if huge movements were emerging in unions that had pareconish norms and values, then yes, they might instruct that their pensions should be spent in productive ways, including in creating pareconish institutions, among other good uses. But again, you can see how that is a process that involves more than one leg, so to speak.

- *What do you think of trying to pass a law that says that corporate polluters, violators of workplace safety, consumer safety, and those convicted of fraud would be taken over, without compensation as penalty, and ownership given to the workers? Since most large corporations eventually do commit such violations, this is essentially a syndicalist proposal. How could you structure this to lead to a parecon?*

I think there is a prior question—what would give any such proposal teeth? If the law was passed tomorrow, virtually the entire economy would be transferrable, immediately, yet none of it would be transferred. A different way of saying this is that if you had movements strong enough to pass the above law, you would have movements strong enough to take over capital on the more positive grounds of desiring a new type of economy. You would also have built those movements over a long period of time, and they would have attained a high level of consciousness and organization already.

But, okay, I will take the hypothesis at face value. Suppose there is a steady transfer, a bit at a time, of private holdings to the workers operating them, for whatever reasons. What additional things would have to occur for this to be a transition to a participatory economy? I think the answer is that (a) the workers would have to be organized locally and within industries into democratic councils. (b) There would have to be a very high consciousness of the need for balanced job complexes and, in general, an elimination of the structural basis for rule by what I call a coordinator class. (c) There would need to be a steady parallel development of a participatory planning apparatus and commitment.

For the transfer of property one needs a movement that is anti-capitalist and strong enough to impose its will against the desires of recalcitrant capitalists to retain their ownership of material assets. For the institution of real council democracy, balanced job complexes, new norms of remuneration, and participatory planning, one needs a movement that has a positive vision and is strong enough to impose its will against the desires of recalcitrant coordinators to retain their relative monopoly on decision making related knowledge, skills, and positions.

17. Participatory Economics

[We seek] a condition of society in which there should be neither rich nor poor, neither master nor master's man, neither idle nor overworked, neither brain-sick brain workers, nor heartsick hand workers, in a word, in which all would be living in equality of condition and would manage their affairs unwastefully, and with the full consciousness that harm to one would mean harm to all—the realization at last of the meaning of the word commonwealth.
-William Morris

Participatory economics is a completely revolutionized economy. Steps we might institute along the way to this goal, ranging from creating workplaces that embody our values to winning better conditions, more power, better information dispersal, better job allocations or other innovations in existing workplaces, are reforms. Reforms can be reformist, when they accept the basic institutions of society and are ends in themselves, with no greater overarching aim in mind. And reforms can be non-reformist, when they seek improvements in current relations, but exist also as self conscious steps in a larger trajectory of on-going change. This book has proposed participatory economics as an economic goal, providing some description of its key features, logic, and virtues. It has answered at least some questions that arise for people on hearing about these new ways of organizing economic life. And it has proposed various programmatic demands and projects which could be strung together as at least part of an agenda of a movement for social change.

A program to attain a participatory economy will inevitably have two broad aspects. One will seek to win innovations within existing institutions, moving them toward pareconish norms and values and providing improvements in people's lives now, as well. The other will seek to create new institutions that are self-consciously implementing as much of the parecon goal as possible in the present, providing schools for understanding and refining our aims, exemplars of those aims, and, again, to better people's lives in the present.

In other words while some people work to create pareconish institutions within the current system, others will work to win changes in power relations and norms within existing institutions, a bit at a time. No one can know in advance what mix and balance of these different methods will ultimately win. My own inclination is to think that building new institutions in the innards of the old is very important for teaching us, raising hopes, keeping our vision clear and forefront, and making us live up to our aspirations, while fighting for changes inside existing structures in ways that build larger and larger movements, increase consciousness, and better the lives of huge numbers of people, is at the heart of organizing. Creating pareconish structures in the present keeps movement building oriented to a worthy future. Movement building for winning non-reformist reforms keeps the creation of vision in the present in touch with the lives and needs of real people. Each provides, or should provide, content and muscle for the other. There is no need for prioritization, nor for competition between the two paths.

This same attitude of mutual solidarity and support should exist as well, as movements develop, between those oriented primarily around economic aims, such as parecon, and those oriented around matters of race, gender, sexuality, political structures, international relations, and ecology. For each particular effort to mature and succeed, they should all be seen as interactive components in one large project for full social justice.

As to the worth of parecon itself and what to do next, the words of Martin Luther King Jr. provide an excellent measuring rod:

"Works are of value only if they give rise to better ones. I have the audacity to believe that peoples everywhere can have three meals a day for their bodies, education and culture for their minds, and dignity, equality, and freedom for their spirits. I believe that what self-centered people have torn down, other-centered people can build up.. ...human progress is neither automatic nor inevitable.... We are now faced with the fact that tomorrow is today. We are confronted with the fierce urgency of NOW. In this unfolding conundrum of life and history there is such a thing as being too late.... this is no time for apathy or complacency. This is a time for vigorous and positive action "

Other Titles by Michael Albert

From his days as an anti-war activist at MIT to the founding of South End Press and *Z Magazine*, Michael Albert has used the scientific model he learned studying physics to expose the injustices which permeate our society, and to offer concrete alternatives to the systems that create them. He is a unique, powerful and underappreciated voice on the left. AK Press distributes these Michael Albert books.

Thinking Forward: Learning To Conceptualize Economic Vision
$13.95 • pb • Arbeiter Ring
1 894037 00 6

A highly accessible and unorthodox approach to thinking about economics. It subverts the elitist and codified world of academic economics by empowering the reader with the tools needed to conceptualize an economy based on progressive and humane values. It challenges the idea - so prevalent in Western capitalism - that the best we can hope for is capitalism with a happy face. And it challenges us to imagine what could be: a society based on justice, solidarity, and vision.

Looking Forward: Participatory Economics in the Twenty-First Century
$16.00 • pb • South End Press
0 89608 405 1

Lavishly illustrated and accessible description of a new type of collectively self-managed, efficient and classless economy.

Stop the Killing Train: Radical Visions for Radical Change
$15.00 • pb • South End Press
0 89608 470 1

Controversial and hard hitting collection of essays from Michael Albert. With a foreword by Noam Chomsky.

Z Magazine and ZNet
http://www.zmag.org

ZNet is the website sponsored and hosted by *Z Magazine*, the print monthly. We have years of articles online, searchable in diverse ways, with monthly tables of contents for more recent entries. We of course have means for you to Subscribe to Z. And we also have various related projects sponsored by or allied with Z including the Parecon Project, South End Press, ZMI, Speak Out, Chomsky Archive, and Alt Radio.

ZNet Creative

ZNet Creative is a facility for ZNet users to enter poetry, short fiction, and lyrics. Enter your own or well known offerings that others will appreciate, or search by topic, author, or keyword through the large store of materials that have been placed by other users. Some related interactive facilities of ZNet are: ZNet Cartoons, where cartoonists enjoying ZNet can share their work with the rest of us; Pen Pals, in which over 1,000 users from all over the world have entered brief biographical information and email addresses to find one another for email exchange; our Socializing facility to help folks get into direct touch with one another; our Calendar to post events and such; and our Quotes Center including a huge store of politically relevant quotes, uploaded by users and searchable by topic.

ZNet Interactive

Use this overarching ZNet InterActive facility to post or view user posted reports, analyses, photos, and links to our highly searchable, user friendly display areas. Topical subsites are created as needed for national demonstrations, etc.

Watch Areas

ZNet's Watch Areas are each subsites unto themselves, sometimes very large, sometimes more modest. They provide essays, reports, and links on the relevant topic often prepared by volunteers for ZNet. The full list of these sites includes: Activism, Algeria, Alt. Media, Anarchy, Animal Rights, Biotechnology, Economy, Foreign Policy, Gender, Global Watch, Ireland, Japan Watch, Labor, Mideast, Parecon, Queer Watch, Race, South Asia, Third Party, and Web Watch.

Current Crises and Struggles

ZNet's Crisis sections each focus on some facet of current struggle, providing links, essays, analyses, etc. Some are modest, others are huge subsites in their own right. Our Crisis sections include: Chiapas/Zapatista, Colombia, East Timor, Global Economics, Iraq, Kosovo, Mumia, Pacifica, Peltier, Puerto Rico, and Russia.

Subsites and Sections

ZNet has many "subsites," each including stores of regularly updated content bearing on some area of activism or concern. One of the most active is our Global Economics Crisis Section. ZNet also regularly creates subsections on the fly for specific events and demonstrations. An example is ZNet's Conventions Coverage pages, from the Summer 2000 political conventions. At any given moment ZNet is likely to have a few subsections dealing with current controversies or exploring some ideas or topics, or debating issues. Here are some examples: AIDS Controversies, Sargent's Adventures in "Feminism," Rationality and Postmodernism Debates, and Libertarian Municipalism Debates.

Topics Links

Yes, ACTIVISTS Do Have (some) Vision and lots of theory and analysis! ZNet includes, for example, topic guides for Political Economy, International Relations, Feminism/Sexuality, Multiculturalism, Third Parties, and Ecology. We have endless collections of links around the web... plus daily updated materials within ZNet itself including articles from our many writers. We have the visionary Parecon Project subsite, about a better economy. We have sections of Interviews and educational Instructionals.

Other Languages

Remarkably, parts of ZNet are being translated to provide access to non-English speaking audiences. Multilingual ZNet includes sections in Korean, Bulgarian, Spanish, French, and Swedish.

For more on
Participatory Economics

Visit the parecon website at
http://www.parecon.org

The parecon website is an effort:
to refine and otherwise improve the parecon vision
to disseminate information about it and build support for it
to stimulate activism around it, and
to provide support for people trying to implement components of parecon

The site includes:
many links to introductory materials.
Frequently Asked Questions
a Participatory Economics Instructional -- a thorough study of parecon ideas, taking advantage of Internet technology to make learning easy.
a set of twelve sequential commentaries on parecon vision AND program.
inks to essays, articles and reviews, all central or relevant to parecon
links to other related web sites.

http://www.parecon.org

New Titles from AK Press

COHN-BENDIT, Daniel & Gabriel
Obsolete Communism : The Left-Wing Alternative
$17.95/£10.00 • pb • AK Press
1 902593 25 1

"Their nightmares are our dreams"

In May 68 a student protest at Nanterre University spread to other universities, to Paris factories and in a few weeks to most of France. On May 13 a million Parisians marched. Ten million workers went out on strike. At the center of the fray from the beginning was Daniel Cohn-Bendit, expelled from Nanterre for his agitation. Obsolete Communism was written in 5 weeks immediately after the French state regained control, and no account of May 68 or indeed of any rebellion can match its immediacy or urgency.

Daniel's gripping account of the revolt is complemented by brother Gabriel's biting criticism of the collaboration of the state, union leadership and the French Communist Party in restoring order, defusing revolutionary energy & handing the factories back to the capitalists. Leninism & the unions come under fire as top-down bureaucracies whose need to manage and control are always at odds with revolutionary action.

"Daniel Cohn-Bendit is the most dangerous scoundrel in France" - President Chas. deGaulle.

MURRAY BOOKCHIN
Anarchism, Marxism and the Future of the Left
$19.95/£13.95 • pb • AK Press
1 873176 35 X
Murray Bookchin has been a dynamic revolutionary propagandist since the 1930s when, as a

teenager, he orated before socialist crowds in New York City and engaged in support work for those fighting Franco in the Spanish Civil War.

Now, for the first time in book form, this volume presents a series of exciting and engaged interviews with, and essays from the founder of social ecology.

This expansive collection ranges over, amongst others, Bookchin's account of his teenage years as a young Communist during the Great Depression; his experiences of the 1960s and reflections on that decade's lessons; his vision of a libertarian communist society; libertarian politics; the future of anarchism; and the unity of theory and practice. He goes on to assess the crisis of radicalism today and defends the need for a revolutionary Left. Finally he states what is to be valued in both anarchism and Marxism in building such a Left, and offers guidelines for forming a new revolutionary social movement.

ALBERT MELTZER
Anarchism: Arguments For and Against
$5.95/£3.95 • pb • AK Press
1 873176 57 0

Everything you wanted to know about anarchism. A new, revised and updated edition of the definitive pocket primer on anarchism. From the historical background and justification of anarchism to the class struggle, organization and role of the anarchist in auhtoritarian society, this sim tome walks the reader through both theory and practice. The book concludes with a set of questions and objections from a variety of political positions: Leninist, Fascist, Social-Democrat, and apolitical Chris on the corner. The perfect introduction for those who wish they were better informed, the mildly curious, and especially those looking for a place to start their new anarchist life. ALBERT MELTZER is the author of I Couldn't Paint Golden Angels: Sixty Years of Commonplace Life and Anarchist Agitation. Emma Goldman described him as a "hooligan and rascal who knows nothing of anarchism." Judge for yourself.

CLEAVER, Harry
Reading Capital Politically
$15.00/£8.00 • pb • AK Press/AntiTheses
1 902593 29 4

As social movements waned in the late 70s, the study of Marx seemed to take on a life of its own. Structuralist, post-structuralist, deconstructed Marxes bloomed in journals and seminar rooms across the United States and Europe. These Marxes and their interpreters struggled to interpret the world, and sometimes to interpret Marx himself, losing sight at times of his dictum that the challenge is not to interpret the world but to change it. In 1979 Harry Cleaver tossed an incendiary device called *Reading Capital Politically* into those seminar rooms. Through a close reading of the first chapter, he shows that Das Kapital was written for the workers, not for academics, and that we need to expand our idea of workers to include housewives, students, the unemployed and other non-waged workers. *Reading Capital Politically* provides a theoretical and historical bridge between struggles in Europe in the 60s & 70s, and particulary the Autonomia of Italy to the Zapatistas of the 90s. Cleaver adds a new preface to the AK Press/Anti-Theses edition.

HO, Fred ed.
Legacy to Liberation: Politics & Culture of Revolutionary Asian/Pacific America
$22.95/£15.95 • pb • AK Press
1 902593 24 3

The Black Panther Party and the Brown Berets live on in our historical memory, but what of the revolutionary groups which came out of Asian America in the late 60s and early 70s? Compiled by veteran and younger Asian Pacific American activist-fighters, from across the U.S. and ideological and political spectrum, Legacy to Liberation is a groundbreaking anthology which documents & analyzes three decades of radical and revolutionary movement building. Penetrating essays interwoven with archival photos, artwork, poetry, and an appendix of rare manifestos, position papers and other documents. Over 30 contributors are featured, including: Ninotchka Rosca, Helen Toribio, Richard Aoki, Yuri Kochiyama, Merle Woo, Nellie Wong, Fred Ho, Steve Yip, Diane Fujino, Dolly Veale & Kent Wong.

New Titles From AK Audio

Spoken Word from Noam Chomsky & Howard Zinn

CHOMSKY, Noam
Case Studies In Hypocrisy: US Human Rights Policy
$20.00/£10.00 • 2 x CD • AK Press
1 902593 27 8

With the recent celebration of the 50th anniversary of the Universal Declaration Of Human Rights, and America's undisputed position as the world's only superpower, the contrast between the rhetoric and reality of US foreign policy has never been more stark. With his penetrating analysis & dry wit, Chomsky leads us through the murky blood-soaked reality of America's New World Order - whether it's NAFTA, GATT, MAI and the WTO or our relations with Palestine, Israel, Haiti and China. The second lecture of this two part set focuses on the motives and consequences of US Iraq policy - a continuing (though hardly unique) shining example of murderous hypocrisy at its most lethal.world of the 'free market' and pulls aside the curtain on these and other capitalist fantasies.

Free Market Fantasies: Capitalism in the Real World
$14.98/£10.00 • compact disc • AK Press
1 873176 79 1

There is endless talk about the free market and its virtues. Entrepreneurs compete on level playing fields and the public benefits. But the chasm between such fantasies and reality is acute and growing. Megamergers and monopolies are limiting 'competition.' Fewer than ten corporations control most of the global media, while the existing free market depends heavily on taxpayer subsidies and bailouts. Corporate welfare grossly exceeds that which goes to the poor. The captains of industry today make the robber barons of the 19th century look like underachievers. The gap between CEO and worker salaries has never been sharper. One union leader put it this way: "Workers are getting the absolute crap kicked out of them." Chomsky takes us into the twisted world of the 'free market' & pulls aside the curtain on these and other capitalist fantasies.

Class War: The Attack On Working People
$12.98/£10.00 • compact disc • AK Press
1 873176 27 9

Corporations and their political allies wage an unrelenting class war against working people. Privatization, the market and level playing fields are the mantras of the day. CEOs tell workers to tighten their belts while their own wallets are bulging. Income inequality is more acute in the US that in any other industrialized country, even surpassing Britain. Glamorous Manhattan has disparities in wealth that exceed Guatemala. People are working longer hours, producing more and earning less. Wages have been stagnant or declining for more than twenty years. The ranks of the poor have mushroomed. Meanwhile profits are at unprecedented levels. 'Class War' is vintage Chomsky. His astute analyses provide excellent tools for self-defense. His commitment, involvement and accessibility are exemplary. It's no wonder that the New Statesman calls him "The conscience of the American people."

Propaganda And Control Of The Public Mind

$20.00/£10.00 • double compact disc • AK Press
1 873176 68 6

"The war against working people should be understood to be a real war. It's not a new war. It's an old war. Furthermore it's a perfectly conscious war everywhere, but specifically in the US...which happens to have a highly class-conscious business class.....And they have long seen themselves as fighting a bitter class war, except they don't want anybody else to know about it." 'There's no doubt that one of the major issues of twentieth century history, surely in the US, is corporate propaganda........Its goal from the beginning, perfectly openly and consciously, was to "control the public mind," as they put it. The reason was that the public mind was seen as the greatest threat to the corporations." [Noam Chomsky, from the CD]

Spin magazine calls him "a capitalist's worst nightmare."

NOAM CHOMSKY/CHUMBAWAMBA
For A Free Humanity: For Anarchy

$18.00/not available in UK • double compact disc • AK Press / Mutual Aid
1 873176 74 0

A Double CD with Noam Chomsky and English anarchist band Chumbawamba. Disc One comprises the Noam Chomsky lecture 'Capital Rules' - another articulate and immediately accessible description of Corporate America's unrelenting attack on poor and working class people. From the attack on unions to the well crafted business propaganda campaigns, Chomsky provides us with a clear picture of how US Capital is leading us down a path of a two tiered society with islands of extreme wealth in a sea of poverty. Disc Two is Chumbawamba's best collection of live sounds - Showbusiness!, previously only available as an expensive import. Recorded live in 94, as a benefit for Anti-Fascist Action, this presents their best material performed the way they do it best. The double CD is accompanied by a 24 page booklet, with extensive interviews with both Noam Chomsky - discussing corporate structure as private tyranny, domestic surveillance of activists, and visions for a new society - and Chumbawamba - discussing their past, politics, and anarchism.

VARIOUS ARTISTS
Monkeywrenching the New World Order

$20.00/£10.00 • 2 x compact disc • AK Press
1 902593 35 9

One year after tens of thousands of demonstrators shut down the World Trade Organization meeting in Seattle, here's an audio compilation introducing the New World Order and its discontents. Featuring the best bits of leading critics and analysts of globalization, including: Noam Chomsky, Alexander Cockburn, Kristin Dawkins, Robin Hahnel, Winona LaDuke, Michael Parenti, Dan Schiller, Vandana Shiva, A Sivanandan, the notorious Acme Collective (part of the Black Block at Seattle), the Biotic Baking Brigade abd more. The CD covers changing politics, militarism and policing, environmental issues, frankenfood and genetic engineering, digital capitalism & the fairy tale economic boom, and the leading alternatives to and struggles against a system which puts profits over people, unregulated growth over sustainability and money over morals.

ZINN, Howard
Stories Hollywood Never Tells
$13.98/£10.00 • CD • AK Press
1 902593 36 7

What sort of view of our history do we get from Hollywood movies? Why are some stories told and others not? Howard Zinn's People's History of the United States helped to enlarge our sense of history to include the stories of women, minorities, labor struggles and others forgotten or removed from official histories. In this informal talk given at the Taos Film Festival, Zinn turns his attention to Hollywood, the stories it tells and the ones it doesn't. He tells the stories of wars from the point of view of disillusioned deserters, of the differences between All Quiet on the Western Front and Saving Private Ryan, of railroad strikes and the Haymarket Affait, Eugene Debs and the real story of Helen Keller, socialist and anti-war agitator. Mother Jones leads a march of 11 and 12-year-old textile workers from Pennsylvania to Roosevelt's vacation home in Oyster Bay to demand better working conditions in the textile mills then at age 85 is thrown in jail for leading the Colorado Coal strike of 1913-4. A spellbinding and provocative talk by America's most beloved historian.

Heroes and Martyrs: Emma Goldman, Sacco & Vanzetti, and the Revolutionary Struggle
$20.00/£10.00 • 2 x CD • AK Press
1 902593 26 X

Howard Zinn takes us back a century to a newly industrialized America, the time of robber barons & tycoons, of tenements bursting with immigrants, of dramatic and often violent labor struggles like Haymarket & Homestead. Zinn's cast includes Cornelius Vanderbilt and Andrew Carnegie, the young J. Edgar Hoover, Oliver Wendell Holmes and George Bernard Shaw. But his focus, as ever, is on the organizers and agitators in the laboring and immigrant communities, a cast as colorful as any novel, like Ben Reitman, the king of the hobos, and Alexander Berkman, author of *Prison Memoirs of an Anarchist*; Nicola Sacco and Bartolomeo Vanzetti, anarchist organizers whose arrest, conviction and execution on trumped-up murder charges produced storms of protest around the world, and Emma Goldman, feminist, anarchist, propagandist extraordinaire for free love and against capitalist exploitation, for direct action and against oppression.

A People's History of the United States: a lecture at Reed College
$20.00/£10.00 • 2 x CD • AK Press
1 873176 95 3

A scintillating lecture & discussion by the legendary teacher, historian and activist. Here Zinn explains with great humor and passion how his teaching, his history and his activism are parts of the same project. The stories of social movements—labor, civil rights, feminism, anti-war—are left out or grossly distorted in mainstream history writing. The efforts of Zinn and others to recover and pass on those stories offer to their students, to their readers and to us, models, ideas, inspirations for how and why we might go about challenging and changing the structures of power.

"What can I say that will in any way convey the love, respect, and admiration I feel for this unassuming hero who was my teacher and mentor." Alice Walker

About AK Press

A K Press Distribution is a workers' co-operative wholly owned by its members. All decisions, including which titles we distribute and what we publish, are made collectively. Our goal is to make available radical books and other materials, titles that are published by independent presses, not the corporate giants, titles with which you can make a positive change in the world. The sorts of books we stock are less and less available from the corporate publishers, booksellers and websites. We urge you to support your local independent booksellers and infoshops. If you don't find our books in the stores, ask for them. You can also order direct from us. You can help us further the dissemination of radical literature by becoming a Friend of AK (see below), encouraging your local bookstores and libraries to order from us, telling your friends about us, volunteering, and creating social revolution.

To order any of the books advertised here, or to receive a free catalog, please contact us at the address below, or check out our website and online catalog at http://www.akpress.org or http://www.akuk.com.

AK PRESS DISTRIBUTION
PO Box 40682
San Francisco, CA 94140
akpress@akpress.org

AK PRESS DISTRIBUTION (UK)
PO Box 12766
Edinburgh EH8 9YE Scotland
ak@akedin.demon.co.uk

FRIENDS OF AK PRESS

In the last 12 months, AK Press published around 10 titles. In the next year, we should be able to do about the same: a cheeky history of insurrection called *Orgasms of History*; new CDs from Mumia Abu-Jamal and Noam Chomsky; *Facing the Enemy*, a biography of Alexander Skirda; a new edition of Cliff Harper's *Anarchy: A Graphic Guide*. Our regular readers will have noticed that some books announced in last year's catalog are still not published. Money is tight, and once the market crashes, the pittance we circulate among ourselves will shrink even further. Working people will be asked again to bail out the rich. The book industry, like the rest of the capitalist world, continues to be a place where the big and rich prosper by devouring the smaller and poorer. Many of the stores to which we sell are suffering as are most of the publishers whose titles we stock. We need your help to make and keep the crucial materials we publish available. With financial help from you, we can publish more books, get them out and into readers' hands sooner. Current projects include: a new Situationist anthology; the first English edition of the complete works of Bakunin (8 vols.); a lively anthology of anarcha-feminist writings; a new translation of Pannekoek on workers' councils; more Vaneigem; CDs from Howard Zinn & Utah Phillips.

The Friends of AK Press is a way in which you can directly help us to realize these and many more such projects. Friends pay a minimum (of course, we have no objection to larger sums) of $15/£10 per month, for a minimum of three months into the AK Press account. Moneys received go directly into our publishing projects. Friends may choose to sign up for a limited period or choose to become ongoing friends. In return, they receive (for the duration of their membership), automatically , as they appear, one FREE copy of EVERY new AK Press title. Secondly they are entitled to a 10% discount on EVERYTHING featured in the AK Press Distribution catalog on ANY and EVERY order. Groups or an individual can also sponsor a whole book. Contact us for details or to sign up.